The Columbia Guide
to Online Style

JANICE R. WALKER
AND TODD TAYLOR

The Columbia Guide to Online Style

Columbia

University

Press

New York

Columbia University Press
Publishers Since 1893
New York   Chichester, West Sussex

Library of Congress Cataloging-in-Publication Data
Walker, Janice R.
    The Columbia guide to online style / Janice R. Walker and Todd Taylor.
    p.   cm.
    Includes bibliographical references and index.
    ISBN 0-231-10788-9 (hardcover : alk. paper) — ISBN 0-231-10789-7
(pbk. : alk. paper)
    1. Authorship—Data processing—Style manuals. 2. Citation of elec-
tronic information sources. I. Taylor, Todd W. II. Title.
PN171.F56W35   1998   98-22875
808'.027—dc21

Casebound editions of Columbia University Press books
are printed on permanent and durable acid-free paper.

Printed in the United States of America

c 10 9 8 7 6 5 4 3 2

p 10 9 8 7 6 5 4 3 2

CONTENTS

PART 1 CITATION

PART 2 PRODUCTION

LIST OF FIGURES

Preface

All standards and guides to style, whether aimed at print or other media, necessarily suffer from the problem of trying to regiment the intractable. This book, then, attempts to achieve the apparently impossible: to provide an authoritative guide to the world of online writing and publishing, a world that continues to morph at such a rate that establishing standards may seem impossible or even deplorable.

The variety and complexity of human communication, even within the relatively coordinated realm of academic discourse, seem too vast to be captured or standardized effectively. Furthermore, some argue that standards, rules, and style guides constrict the creative expressions of authors. In fact, many proponents of online writing and electronic publication are specifically encouraged by the prospect that the new media will lead to a radical disruption of the conventions and traditions of print publication. Such arguments are worth noting; however, standards can be as liberating as they are limiting. Authors and publishers who seek a voice within a specific discourse community often want and need to follow the conventions and speak the language of their audience. Not only do conventions and specialized vocabularies provide the utilitarian mechanisms through which communication can take place, they also play a crucial role in simultaneously reflecting, promoting, and defining the values and identity of particular discourse communities. In other words, effective style is not an imposed artifice; it is a product of common values, to the degree that such values can be determined.

Because the spectrum of human communications is vast, this style guide, like others, can address with authority only a small segment of it: the production of academic discourse in the form of student and professional papers and reports and scholarly work for publication. It describes standards for academic authors and publishers who want to produce research that is straightforward in terms of traditional, print-oriented content and format, even though such work is composed, stored, and accessed electronically.

This book stresses the importance of the connections between style and scholarly integrity, connections on which all academic disciplines rely. Currently, literally hundreds of published style guides for citing resources and producing texts reflect the particular values and conventions of individual disciplines and specializations within academe. As diverse as these groups may be, however, they all share common concerns. Yet too often manuals present style as a decontextualized catechism of rules to be observed, whereas its primary aim is to promote scholarly integrity. Many people operate under the misguided notion that style is primarily a means to ensure that authors and publishers receive appropriate intellectual and financial credit for their work and to subjugate initiates in academic discourse. It would be foolish to deny that such impulses are associated with the promulgation of academic style. Nevertheless, the preeminent goal of style is to support the continuous, communal, and cross-generational process of knowledge building. Style is one very important mechanism that helps facilitate this process.

Many have suggested that the mind-boggling explosion of electronic discourse—primarily as the result of word processing, desktop publishing, and Internet technologies—presents a "threat" to scholarly integrity because it promises to upset long-established conventions and traditions. Yet scholarship, scholarly integrity, and style are more likely to shift and become redefined than to evaporate as more and more work is published online instead of on paper. In other words, if scholarship is to make a successful transition from print to electronic media, as most believe it will, new standards for ensuring scholarly integrity online must be established.

Tellingly, this book is not so much the result of the authors trying to bottle the ether as much as the ether itself demanding a bottle. In 1994 Janice Walker quietly and somewhat naively developed a simple but highly effective style sheet for citing online resources. The style sheet was quickly endorsed by the Alliance for Computers and Writing, became known as the Walker/ACW Style Sheet, and was published on the World Wide Web (WWW). Soon after, Walker was bombarded with hundreds of requests from libraries, universities, associations, and publishers for permission to use and duplicate her style sheet. And after *The Chronicle of Higher Education, Internet World, USA Today,* and *Newsweek* featured the Walker/ACW style sheet in their publications, countless writers, scholars, and researchers contacted her, encouraging her to expand this work.

Other historical events also played a role. Between 1993 and 1995, all three of the leading authorities on academic style (APA, Chicago, and MLA) published long-awaited and newly revised editions of their style guides, all three explicitly promising to provide authoritative standards addressing the latest changes brought on by the advent of electronic media. Yet the very timing of the new editions prevented them from establishing such standards. While the Internet or its predecessors had been in place since the late 1960s, a monumental expansion of online technologies into mainstream academic and popular culture took place between 1993 and 1994, precisely the time at which the APA, Chicago, and MLA style guides were in production or being printed. The result was that none of the three guides captured the crucial changes brought on by the WWW. Because of the simplicity of creating and storing information on the WWW as well as the global accessibility it offers, online publishing seems to have arrived at a period of relative stability, at least in the sense that even though technology continues to change daily, the WWW provides the first glimpse of an infrastructure that promises to support reasonable levels of online scholarly integrity. Clearly, much remains to be done if most new research and scholarship is one day to be published online. One major obstacle is the reliability of the infrastructure. Who is going to ensure that the Internet is stable and reliable and not a nightmare of bottlenecks? Will corporations or governments provide such reliability? Who will organize, index, and provide long-term archives for online scholarship? Will university libraries supply these services? Who will oversee the prudent evolution of other mechanisms important to online scholarly integrity, such as peer review? Will university presses and journal editors do this work?

Even while such questions are being answered, we can begin establishing and promoting standards for the production of conventional academic publications through electronic media, standards that should help support the eventual development of reliable infrastructures. Two important caveats regarding such standards must be addressed, however. First, even though this book is a guide to more or less traditional forms of scholarship published online, scholars should at least consider exploring experimental forms that fall outside the scope of our project. Experiments in online publishing such as hypertextual indexes and interactive footnotes already demonstrate some of the ways online documents can greatly improve on conventional print-oriented styles. Refusing to encourage and take advantage of such experiments is clearly a threat to scholarly integrity.

The second caveat speaks to the style of this book itself. At first it may seem that this guide to online style is bound by the limitations of print publishing. How can the reader expect to rely on the standards it describes given that electronic publishing technologies will change even as this book is in press or between editions? The answer is that this "book" is actually only part of a larger project known as *The Columbia Guide to Online Style,* which involves continuous online updates to address necessary revisions to the print edition you are currently reading. The core standards promoted in this book—for citing most online resources, providing in-text citations, and for producing electronic documents— will not change dramatically in most cases. Online updates will most likely address nonmainstream issues such as standards for documenting an emerging but not yet widely used type of document. Modifications to the print edition are available online for free (at http://www.columbia.edu/cu/cup/cgos/); most academic libraries will have copies of the updates if you are unable to access them yourself.

✳ ✳ ✳

The authors wish to acknowledge the departments of English at the University of South Florida, Tampa, and the University of North Carolina, Chapel Hill, for their support. We also want to thank Jennifer Crewe, Anne McCoy, Ron Harris, Mary Ellen Burd, Sarah St. Onge, and the anonymous manuscript reviewers for their enormous help developing the manuscript and preparing this book. This book is truly a coauthored work, with both Janice Walker and Todd Taylor contributing equally to its development and publication. However, since one name inevitably had to precede the other, the authors agreed that Walker's name should be listed first because she had already established the "Walker/ACW Style for Citation of Electronic Sources" before the authors decided to write this book; the term "first author" does not apply to this book in any other sense.

Introduction
Bottling the Ether

The world of online writing evolves so quickly and is of such vital importance that it requires a specialized guide, one that focuses primarily on this complex dimension of academic writing instead of trying to do everything at once, as other style guides attempt to do. *The Columbia Guide to Online Style* is such a tool, a comprehensive guide to citing and producing academic documents and resources that are stored electronically. Working as an interdisciplinary template that can be applied to a variety of already established style guides such as APA, Chicago, and MLA, it offers advice that can be adapted to whichever style a particular discipline, instructor, colleague, journal, editor, or publisher has selected.

The Columbia Guide employs a unique element-oriented approach to style that allows readers to adapt its information and standards to a wide variety of situations. The overarching principle behind the element approach is that although different academic communities have different ways of ordering, punctuating, and even spelling the various elements that constitute, for example, a bibliographic reference, they almost universally make use of the exact same elements of style: the author's name, title of chapter or article, title of book, publisher, date, etc. This guide shows users which elements of online documentation are necessary and important, how to locate them, and, in general, how to present them in both humanities and scientific styles. In the rare case that an author needs to follow a style not covered in this book, he or she can still apply the principles outlined here.

A typical entry in a scientific bibliography might look like this:

Humm, M. (1992). History of feminism in Britain and America. In M. Humm (Ed.), *Modern feminisms: Political, literary, cultural* (pp. 1–15). New York: Columbia UP.

The same information in a humanities bibliography could look like this:

Humm, Maggie. "History of Feminism in Britain and America." In *Modern Feminisms: Political, Literary, Cultural.* Ed. Maggie Humm. New York: Columbia UP, 1992. 1–15.

Comparing the way the styles treat each element reveals the differences between the two. For one thing, the author-date style abbreviates the author's first and middle names, while the humanities style spells these names out completely as provided by authors in the original texts. The author-date style places the date after the author's name, at the beginning of the citation, while the humanities style locates it toward the end. Scientific style dictates that book and article or chapter titles begin with initial capitals only, while in the humanities, titles are capitalized according to traditional standards. The placement of page numbers, the use of quotation marks, and the way in which editors are identified are just some of the other elements that the two styles handle differently.

Why the differences, and why can't everyone agree on a standard approach for all academic writing? The answer is that different disciplines and different communities of writers who operate under the large umbrella of academic writing have different values and different identities. Scientific citation styles aim to promote clinical objectivity and reliance on the very latest data. Thus these styles abbreviate the first names of authors at least in part because doing so seems to suppress the subjective identity of researchers, thereby enhancing their apparent clinical objectivity. The date of publication is foregrounded because it generally matters *when* the research was conducted—the scientific method relies on the latest knowledge or data. In the humanities, by contrast, research and scholarship are more often a matter of *who* said what rather than *when* it was said. Thus humanities-oriented citation styles highlight the names of authors by spelling them out completely, whereas the date of publication, while still important, is located at the end of a citation.

Focusing on generic elements becomes especially important when considering online style. In terms of both citation and production, online documents present often subtle and sometimes profound variations on conventional elements. For instance, in almost every established academic style, the author's name occupies a prominent position. What happens when this key element is missing or difficult to find? Most citation styles suggest that in such cases one simply must list as much other information as appropriate or possible. This is acceptable when such omissions are rare. The problem is that such elements are frequently missing in electronic documents. The cause of this problem is primarily two-fold. First, producers of online academic texts frequently approach such work as prototypic and experimental; they often consciously try to break with academic conventions and disrupt traditional notions of textuality. One of the conventions to which many challenges are being made is the notion of sole authorship. Many online texts are extensively collaborative, making it difficult or impossible to identify authors or even editors in a conventional sense. Second, to date, academic online writing has lacked standards and a stable infrastructure of journals, editors, archives, and publishers to promote even minimal uniformity and reliability among online texts. Because online writers are typically islands unto themselves—acting simultaneously as authors, editors, and publishers—they reinvent online style with each new document. If the production and dissemination of online academic writing is truly to redefine scholarship, it must first successfully negotiate a transitional period of legitimization, a transition that has not yet taken place, as evidenced by the widespread lack of formal and de facto endorsement by academic institutions of online scholarship as serious work.

Standardization of online style is a necessary first step toward negotiating this transition. So far there have been a few attempts to address citation of electronic resources, but none of these has combined a comprehensive examination of citation with extensive advice on production as *The Columbia Guide to Online Style* does. You can't cite effectively if there are no standards for producing scholarly documents in the first place. And there would probably be little reason to produce documents if standardized systems of citation were not in place to give structure to the process of knowledge building. Citation and production are, in essence, reciprocating mechanisms of the larger engine known as academic style. Consequently, this book is divided into two parts, the first of which addresses online citation, while the second part examines online production. The book concludes with an annotated glossary of terms associated with the online world.

Part 1 is divided into two chapters. Chapter 1 examines, in broad and theoretical terms, the logic of citation; it answers the questions, "Why cite?" "Why use a citation style?" Chapter 2 answers the question, "How should we cite online material?" It first provides a guide to citation for authors working with humanities-oriented texts and then discusses an author-date citation system typically used in the sciences.

Part 2 includes four chapters. Chapter 3 discusses the logic— the why—of document style. Chapters 4 and 5 describe standards for how to produce print and online documents. Chapter 6 discusses some more advanced considerations related to online style.

Readers will typically choose to consult chapter 4 or 5, depending on the medium in which they are being asked to submit work and the medium in which the work will ultimately be published. Chapter 4 covers guidelines for using a word processor to create a paper or hard-copy final product (students who must submit conventional papers will most likely want to follow this chapter) and establishes standards for authors who want to furnish editors or publishers with an electronic version of a manuscript (of importance to scholarly authors, editors, and publishers who need both hard copy and electronic copy for efficient editing and production). Chapter 5 presents standards for documents published on computer networks; authors intending to place their work on the World Wide Web should follow these guidelines.

Because *The Columbia Guide to Online Style* addresses a wide range of new standards for citing and producing academic texts, authors must determine which specific portions of the book they should follow. Most academic authors must shape their work with a specific audience in mind and identify and follow the conventions that will appeal to that audience. In most cases, a writer or editor will simply need to refer to the numbered items in chapter 2 for citation and either chapter 4 or 5 for answers to questions concerning online document style. You must make certain, however, that you follow the guidelines required by your readers. If you are a writer in English studies, for example, you should not assume that you should always use a humanities-oriented citation style and only submit your work on paper. Instructors and editors in the humanities may very well prefer an author-date citation style and require manuscripts in Hypertext Markup Language (HTML) format for dissemination over the World Wide Web (chapter 5). Thus authors will often need to ask their instructors, editors, or publishers which conventions they prefer and then select the appropriate chapters in this guide.

If you need to follow a specific academic style that falls outside the examples given in these chapters, we suggest that you first consult the guidelines in chapters 2, 4, or 5 in order to identify which elements of either citation or production are required for effective online style. Next, you may want to examine the specific discussions in chapter 2 of different elements such as author, title, or even page numbers. You may also want to locate in the index other potentially relevant discussions of various elements. Extrapolating the principles outlined in *The Columbia Guide* in order to adhere to a particular academic style should then be a matter of superficial formatting in terms of abbreviation, spelling, punctuation, and ordering of various elements. If this is not the case, we encourage you to contact the authors of this guide through email at cgos@columbia.edu so that we can add your problem to our collection of considerations for updates. Feedback from readers will continue to shape the future of *The Columbia Guide to Online Style.*

PART 1

Citation

1

The Logic
of Citation

What is citation, and why do academics agree to use structured rules for it? Citation is the practice of systematically indicating the origins of thoughts, ideas, or knowledge that one uses to author a report, essay, article, or book (or Web site). Why do people cite? The key to understanding the logic behind citation is understanding the systems upon which it is based. Those who believe the primary purpose of citation is to monitor and police authors misunderstand the logic of the practice. Many have learned to perceive citation as a series of difficult rules employed solely to counter plagiarism, to ensure that authors and publishers of original work receive proper intellectual and financial credit for their work, and even to subjugate new initiates in the world of academic writing. And in all fairness, such misperceptions are not completely the fault of those who see citation in such a negative light. To date, most guides to academic style have not done a good job of explaining *how* to cite in terms of *why* one should do so.

The big picture is about knowledge building: each piece of reported research adds to the collective construction of knowledge. Research serves as the foundation on which new contributions to knowledge are built. Without citation, there is no reliable and organized system for knowledge building, no mortar for securing the foundation. Knowledge building is, of course, not as straightforward as stacking bricks. If academic knowledge were a build-

ing, the structure would be impressive indeed, but—far from being flawless, complete, or symmetrical—its parts would con-
stantly be crumbling and being rebuilt, with scores of different
construction crews with different architectural styles and blue-
prints at work on different parts at the same time.

If the primary reason for citation is that it encourages and supports the organized accumulation of academic knowledge, this
principle has literally hundreds of ramifications. Consider, for example, the fact that most scholars approach bibliographies more
in terms of the knowledge they generate than the strictures they
enforce. Most academic writers will be familiar with the concept
of *bibliography* in the most general sense of the term. A bibliography is a list of works that a writer has consulted in the creation of
a new work. In its most familiar format, this list of works is usually found at the end of an academic document. Writers who mis-
perceive the logic of citation often approach bibliographies with a
sense that an imagined or sometimes real-life authority (perhaps
a teacher or an editor) is peering over their shoulder, threatening
punishment if the rules for compiling and formatting are not followed precisely. Scholars, however—the people most actively in-
volved in academic knowledge building—tend to perceive bibliographies in a very different light. They sometimes read bibliographies with as much interest as they study the work itself because
bibliographies and citations contain crucial information that gen-
erates additional opportunities in the pursuit of knowledge building. Of course, one cannot expect that all writers, especially students, will immediately learn to read and appreciate bibliographies as experienced or full-time scholars do. But inexperienced
writers are more likely to comprehend, appreciate, use, and possibly even master citation if they understand its primary purpose.

Why does a consideration of online style warrant a (re)consid-
eration of the logic of citation and the mechanisms of knowledge
building? A discussion of the problems and misperceptions of in-

experienced writers may seem remedial to those who have been in the business of research and scholarship for years. However, we suggest that we are *all* inexperienced writers and readers of online scholarship because it simply hasn't been around long enough for anyone to have developed the deeply ingrained intuitions that are at work in the world of print scholarship. Changing technology requires us to focus attention on the origins of citation, which have become blurred by years of mere replication without sincere interrogation into the practices of our predecessors in academic discourse. Thus, like novice writers working for the first time with academic writing in print form, inexperienced writers of online scholarship are more likely to comprehend, appreciate, use, and possibly even master online citation if they understand and consider its underlying logic.

Five Principles of Citation Style

The Principle of Access

Citation styles help readers locate with ease the original documents to which authors referred in preparing their own work. The principle of access has many ramifications. Access is valuable so that readers can make use of and build on the sources that an author has discovered; it helps readers evaluate the author's reliability by allowing them to examine the contexts from which the author selected citations. Part of evaluating an author's reliability is being able to verify that work has been cited appropriately and credit has not been taken for ideas or research established by someone else. Subcorollaries under the principle of access require that citation style not just facilitate access but do so with a high degree of efficiency. This means a reader should be able to locate a cited source quickly and with minimal effort. Many existing style guides fail to support the principle of access and its corollaries when it comes to online sources because they do not help readers locate many electronic sources efficiently. For example, the fourth edition of the *MLA Handbook for Writers of Research Papers* (1995) states "you may add as supplementary information the electronic address you used to access the [electronic] document" (sec. 4.9.3, p. 165). Yet the electronic address is essential information for accessing most documents on networks such as the Internet: this information cannot be omitted if a reader is to be able to access the source.

The Principle of Intellectual Property

Using someone else's ideas, words and phrases, or form of presentation without giving proper credit is plagiarism and can carry serious academic as well as legal penalties. Our conception of plagiarism is based on the notion of ownership of intellectual property. In the United States, the logic behind the principle of intellectual property is based on an economic model, stemming from the Constitution's call to "promote the Progress of Science and useful Arts, by securing for limited Times to Authors and Inventors the exclusive Right to their respective Writings and Discoveries" (part. 1, sec. 8, col. 8). Under federal copyright law, words and their form of presentation must be "fixed" in order to be copyrightable. Ideas themselves cannot be copyrighted; only their embodiment has economic value.

Is the Internet a fixed medium? It does have an infrastructure, albeit one that may not be readily apparent to those not familiar with the cyberterrain. Internet protocols and addresses—URLs, FTP, gopher, Telnet, and so on—can usually provide the knowledgeable reader with sufficient information to locate a source. Thus standards of citation should govern in this medium just as in any other wherein the principle of intellectual property must be honored.

The Principle of Economy

Citation style should include as much information as necessary but be as brief as possible so readers can quickly grasp the information they need and publishers can conserve costs incurred in terms of paper, ink, and their employees' time. The following prose approach to citation obviously violates the principle of economy:

> The passage I quote is from an excellent book titled *Modern Feminisms: Political, Literary, Cultural*. The book was edited by Maggie Humm. The passage I cite was located in chapter 1, "History of Feminism in Britain and America"; Humm authored the chapter herself. Chapter 1 can be found on pages 1–15. The book was published in 1992 by Columbia University Press, which is located in New York City, if you need to contact them.

This example is clearly annoying, a waste of time and space as compared with a conventional citation containing similar but only essential information:

MLA STYLE

> Humm, Maggie. "History of Feminism in Britain and America." In *Modern Feminisms: Political, Literary, Cultural*. Ed. Maggie Humm. New York: Columbia UP, 1992. 1–15.

APA STYLE

> Humm, M. (1992). History of feminism in Britain and America. In M. Humm (Ed.), *Modern feminisms: Political, literary, cultural* (pp. 1–15). New York: Columbia UP.

Following the principle of economy, each of these citation styles reduces a potentially lengthy explanation to its essential elements, following a code whereby important information such as the title of a book, the name of its editor, and the pages on which a particular chapter is located are indicated through formatting.

Formatting can be defined as the typographical arrangement and appearance of textual elements: the physical appearance of letters and words on a page, screen, surface, and so on. The most common devices used to format citations are punctuation, font style, and ordering of elements. The use of punctuation in the form of quotation marks placed around a title is a formatting code that usually tells the reader that what is enclosed is the title of an essay, article, or chapter. Using underlining or italics as opposed to a normal font style is a code that typically indicates the title of a journal, report, or book. Placing the name of the editor of a book immediately after the book's title is a code indicating that the editor is not the author of the chapter cited.

The Principle of Standardization

A comparison between the lengthy prose citation and the codified citations above also explains a fourth corollary of citation style: authors and readers must both understand the code being used; therefore that code must be standardized. Consider, for example, the following codified message:

Columbia University Press
562 West 113th Street
New York, NY 10025

The standardization of this code allows everyone to understand its meaning. We all know that this is a mailing address, and that the Columbia University Press is the addressee, which can receive mail sent to a building numbered 562 on West 113th Street in the city of New York in the state of New York, and that the five-digit ZIP code helps postal services deliver mail to that address more efficiently.

Like citation style, the code for indicating a mailing address makes use of punctuation, formatting, and ordering. It is so widely recognized because it always follows explicit standards. In the same way, if authors and readers are to use citation style to support effective knowledge building, they must understand and employ the standards on which the codified style is based.

The Principle of Transparency

This principle presumes that citation style should be as transparent, or as intuitive, as possible, so that as many people as possible will be able to understand its codes. For example, under the principle of economy one could argue that the abbreviation "Ed." isn't absolutely necessary before the second instance of the name "Maggie Humm" in the above examples because one may deduce that "editor" is Humm's most likely supplemental role. However, the principle of transparency maintains that the code or abbreviation "Ed." is probably worth the space it consumes because its presence makes it more likely that the citation will be transparent and thus more widely understood.

Reconsidering the Principles of Citation Online

Differences between the world of print and online publication require that we reconsider the principles of access, intellectual property, economy, standardization, and transparency. The principle of access, for instance, presents some intriguing challenges for citation in online documents. Attempting to ensure the verifiability of a writer's sources, while a worthwhile goal, involves problems of archiving, limited computer resources, and sometimes insufficient knowledge of protocols, which may preclude many authors from providing reliable annotation. Dating electronic files will not guarantee that previous versions will remain accessible. And encouraging authors to retain copies of sources they have referenced could violate current copyright laws. The impossibility of legislating to an international community further complicates this issue online.

As with print-based publications, the principle of access maintains that a citation style should make access to cited online sources as efficient as possible. Should scholarship stored on the World Wide Web (WWW) therefore use hypertextual links to connect a quotation or a paraphrased idea to its original source if the original source is also located online? If so, are bibliographic footnotes or endnotes necessary or a waste of space and effort? If readers can link directly to the original source, then providing notes would be a violation of the principle of economy. On the other hand, that principle might not seem as important when publishing online because the demands of electronic memory storage and distribution are typically insignificant compared with the financial and environmental costs of mass-produced ink-and-paper texts. But what about the principle of standardization? Allowing automatic hypertextual links to replace standard bibliographic references may disrupt the standardized code on which academic readers have relied. Some readers of online work may not recognize or understand the nature of the hypertextual links to cited sources and may still look instead for bibliographic entries or, worse yet, not recognize that a quotation or paraphrase is being cited. Yet under the principle of transparency, hypertextual citation is nearly ideal in that it almost completely eliminates the need to decipher a code in order to access the original source. But, then again, could complete transparency begin to work against the principle of access and the overarching aim of knowledge building? On the WWW, documents tend to be published and vanish more quickly than do printed library books and academic journals. If an author relies solely on hypertextual links to refer to sources cited on the WWW, what happens if the cited source is eventually removed from the Web? Wouldn't a conventional bibliography provide a reasonable level of access while preventing some of the problems with a citation style that is too transparent?

Reconsidering the principle of intellectual property represents one of the most controversial and thorny issues surrounding on-line publication. Books, periodicals, films, audio recordings, and software programs are fixed on a physical medium. But what happens when they move online? Current law stipulates that material protected by copyright must be fixed in some tangible medium. Are documents and journals on the WWW fixed? Is the online world a tangible medium? When do electronic files become fixed? When they are saved to a hard drive or diskette? When they are printed out? What about files that are stored and read entirely on-line, such as electronic mail? And what about the inherent mutability of online writing?

Most World Wide Web documents are still being written and read by people raised and educated in a linear, print-based world. But online writing already means incorporating more than just words in our arrangements; we must now also consider the impact of links, graphics, animation, audio files, and video files, as well as typographical elements such as fonts and white space. We may someday be able to include even smell and taste and touch in our compositions. Still, the shift to a paperless age will not happen overnight, and although more and more of us are now beginning to write online, many of these works are still being written with print formats in mind. Additionally, many texts written for print formats are simply being pasted on to the Net. Formats for citing both electronic and traditional print sources therefore need to be readable in both print and electronic formats. And as the Internet continues to grow and change and we become more comfortable with reading and writing online, any guidelines we adopt will need to be flexible.

But for now the guidelines presented in this book will provide sufficient documentation for print as well as electronic sources. Various discipline-specific style manuals give precise guidelines for citing different types of publications, including books, newspapers, journals, magazines, film clips, and more. When appropriate, authors will need to consult these manuals in addition to the present guide. For electronic sources, however, the examples here will illustrate how to cite elements in the manner required by other styles. For files and documents unique to electronic versions, we have followed the same logic as for more traditional print sources, while recognizing the unique structure of electronic works. And for those electronic sources not addressed here or yet to be developed, our guidelines should nonetheless help readers identify and cite the various elements necessary to give credit adequately.

The more conversational nature of much writing on the Internet adds to the complexity of the transition from print-based to online writing. Scholarship has for some time been described metaphorically as a conversation, an institution that often appears to follow a dialogic progression. In the online world, however, the notion of scholarship as conversation is no longer metaphorical. Electronic mail files (email), newsgroup and listserv postings, File Transfer Protocol (FTP) sites, gopher files, discussions in MUDs (Multi-User Dungeons or Domains), IRC (Internet Relay Chat) discussions, graphics files, audio files, chat rooms, software programs, and even video games may all contain valuable information, and all this information needs to be cited in a way that follows the five principles of citation. Documentation serves as a sort of "he said," "she said," with the "Works Cited" or "References" identifying the speakers. Providing readers with access to sources allows them to enter into the larger conversation.

The conversational nature of writing is readily apparent on the hypertextual World Wide Web, where collaboration is common. Works may become truly multiauthored, and readers may begin or end texts at any point. Identifying authors, titles, dates of publication, and page numbers may become difficult or impossible. When a title *is* provided, how can we know how to punctuate it? How can we tell if an online document is an article or a monograph? How can we guide a reader to the source of a quotation that is drawn from a 100,000-word document with no page numbers? The ease of downloading or capturing text and graphics files makes copying all too easy, and most programs do not automatically capture or record the information necessary for documentation. Sometimes documenting a source may require substantial detective skills. Yet these difficulties should not cause readers and writers to limit themselves to those works that are stable or fixed. Doing so would only curtail their ability to participate fully in the global conversation of the electronic age. Clearly, however, we need standards not only for citing online documents but also for formatting them in the first place.

2

Citing Electronic Sources

The primary elements of a bibliographic reference are the same for most styles of documentation, although the order in which they are presented may vary. Throughout this chapter, we will give examples of citations according to, first, a humanities style based on the MLA criteria and then a scientific style based on APA criteria (the MLA and APA systems being two of the most popular formats in humanities and scientific publishing, respectively). Punctuation should be inserted according to the models shown in the examples. For other styles, the specific elements of online citations can be translated following these guidelines. Whichever style is followed, however, a citation will include acknowledgment of the author, the title of the article or file, the title of the complete work, publication information— usually including place of publication, publisher's name, and the date of publication—and the page number(s) of the article or chapter, if applicable. References in the body of the text usually include the author's last name and the page number for the cited passage; in scientific citation styles, the year of publication is provided as well. The purpose of an in-text citation is to identify the exact location within a document where the specific reference can be found and to point to the full citation in the list of works cited. Citing print resources is not always straightforward, but for the most part, most of the necessary information can be furnished.

For electronic sources, however, some elements may be missing or must be translated into elements that make sense in a new era of publishing. When in doubt, it is better to give too much information than too little.

THE ELEMENTS OF CITATION

2.1 Authorship

Providing the URL (Uniform Resource Locator) or Internet address is the key element in citing electronic sources, since this will allow the best chance of locating a source, provided it still exists. Documents in cyberspace, whether text files, graphic files, audio files, or other types of files, often have no clear designation of authorship, but the electronic address or URL may include a pointer to the author in the directories included in the Internet address after the domain name. However, because this information is already included in the citation as part of the document address and the designation may refer to the Internet "publisher" rather than the author, documents with no apparent author should be listed by the title of the page.

The International Standards Organization (ISO) requires that the person or persons with "primary responsibility" for a referenced site be cited. Of course, the author is usually the person with primary responsibility. But, as with any kind of scholarship, those who contributed to the production of the work—including editors, compilers, translators, and so forth—may need to be given credit as well. Yet many electronic files do not include any identification whatsoever of the author or other contributors. Online authors may also use aliases—either fictitious names or login names—and although this practice is centuries old, we often tend to view anonymous electronic works with suspicion. Academic authors should be encouraged to identify their work plainly, and chapter 5 gives suggestions for accomplishing this in hypertextual documents (see sections 5.1 and 5.1.1). However, discounting work simply because the author is unknown is not a viable alternative. If some information is not available, then the only choice is to give whatever information you can.

2.1.1 Login Names

In figure 2.1, the only designation of the author is the email address, jwalker@chuma.cas.usf.edu.

For documentation purposes, you will use whatever name is available.

HUMANITIES STYLE

The bibliographic citation for the email in figure 2.1 would read:

jwalker. "Electronic Mail Headers." Personal email (16 Aug. 1996).

SCIENTIFIC STYLE

Personal correspondence is not usually included in the list of references; instead, it is cited within the body of the text. Other types of email messages, however, such as postings to a newsgroup or listserv, should be cited following the same principle described above. For example, an email message sent to a listserv would read:

jwalker. Electronic mail headers. walker-l@nosferatu.cas.usf.edu (16 Aug. 1996).

Date: Fri, 16 Aug 1996 10:09:23 -0400 (EDT)
From: jwalker@chuma.cas.usf.edu
To: moxley@chuma.cas.usf.edu
Subject: Electronic Mail Headers

Figure 2.1 An Electronic Mail Header

2.1.2 Aliases or Fictitious Names

In synchronous communication sites, such as MUDs (Multi-User Dungeons, or Domains) and IRC (Internet Relay Chat), users can choose fictitious names, or the database may randomly assign them "guest" names. For instance, ChibaMOO assigns guests character names such as Pine_Guest, Loblolly_Guest, and Spruce_ Guest (guest names at this site are all types of trees), while characters (users who have obtained accounts on the system) can choose character names, such as Kiwi, Spring, or Fenris_Ulf. Even at MediaMOO, where scholars in computers and writing meet in real time to discuss various issues, characters have names such as JaniceW, true, and barrym. To cite these conversations, you will use whatever information is available. For example:

HUMANITIES STYLE

JanetC. "Computer Questions and Answers for Writing Teachers." *Netoric's Tuesday Cafe.* 6 Feb. 1996. ftp://ftp.daedalus.com/pub/ACW/NETORIC/Tuesday_Cafe_log. 06Feb (16 Aug. 1996).

SCIENTIFIC STYLE

JanetC. (1996, February 6). Computer questions and answers for writing teachers. *Netoric's Tuesday Cafe.* ftp://ftp.daedalus.com/pub/ACW/NETORIC/Tuesday_Cafe_log. 06Feb (16 Aug. 1996).

2.1.3 Signature Files

Some electronic mail headers may include the full name of the author, or the message may contain a "signature file" that indicates the author's full name. Figure 2.2 gives the author's name, "Janice Walker," as well as the email address in the header. The signature

Date: Fri, 16 Aug 1996 10:09:23 -0400 (EDT)
From: "Janice Walker (ENG)" <jwalker@chuma.cas.usf.edu>
To: walker-l@nosferatu.cas.usf.edu
Subject: Signature Files

In addition to designating the full names of the author and the recipient in the email header, this message contains a "signature file" which gives further information about the author.

****
Janice R. Walker, Dept. of English   Email jwalker@chuma.cas.usf.edu
University of South Florida   Tampa, FL (813) 974-2421
                http://www.cas.usf.edu/english/walker/janice.html
          HURRY! ONLY ONE DAY LEFT UNTIL TOMORROW!
****

Figure 2.2 An Electronic Mail Message with Author Name and Signature File

file at the end of the message gives additional information about the author.

The bibliographic citation for this message in humanities style would read:

> Walker, Janice. "Signature Files." walker-l@nosferatu.cas.usf.edu (16 Aug. 1996).

In scientific style, the author's first name is omitted and only the initial or initials are listed, the quotation marks around the title of the article are omitted, and only the first word of the title is capitalized. No parenthetical date is included after the author's name when the message date and the access date are the same:

> Walker, J. Signature files. walker-l@nosferatu.cas.usf.edu (16 Aug. 1996).

Note that personal email messages are not included in reference lists in either style: publishing someone's email address would be like publishing a home address or phone number. The email address that is included is the address of the public listserv or newsgroup where the message is "published."

2.1.4 Other Identifying Information

Some synchronous communication sites may allow you to access information about participants. You may choose to cite the author's name rather than an alias or login name if that information is publicly available. Many electronic files do not list an author's name (or names) but may include the name of the person responsible for compiling or maintaining the site. These names may be cited following the same principles applied in citations listing editors or translators of print works. For example:

HUMANITIES STYLE

Doherty, Mick, comp. "Electronic Feedback: *CMC Magazine* Visits the Netoric Cafe." *Computer-Mediated Communication Magazine* 2.3 (1995): 41. http://sunsite.unc.edu/cmc/mag/1995/mar/netoric. html (10 Aug. 1996).

SCIENTIFIC STYLES

The abbreviation "Comp." (for compiler) is included in parentheses following the name:

Doherty, M. (Comp.). (1995). Electronic feedback: *CMC Magazine* visits the Netoric Cafe. *Computer-Mediated Communication Magazine, 2*(3), 41. http://sunsite.unc.edu/cmc/mag/1995/mar/netoric.html (10 Aug. 1996).

As in print sources, sites may also be authored by corporate or government agencies; video and audio files may include information about composers, producers, or performers; or online sites may include the names of translators or editors. Follow the same principles as outlined in your style manual for print sources, translating electronic elements as necessary following the guidelines presented in this chapter.

2.2 Publication Information

Many Internet documents and files are brief, and it is often difficult or impossible to ascertain if they are part of a larger body of work or can be considered to be independently published. If you know that a page is part of a larger work published online, then you should designate it as such. Cite a book or journal published online or on CD-ROM or through another electronic medium just as you would a print publication, italicizing the title and including any volume, issue, or page numbers, if applicable. In general, however, online publications represent unique editions; thus the usual print publication information (e.g., place of publication and publisher's name) should be replaced by the electronic protocol and address (for Internet sources) or the name of the online service provider or database, as appropriate. For example, to cite a book published on the World Wide Web (WWW), include the author's name; the book title, in italics; the date of publication (if known); the protocol and address; and the date accessed.

HIIMANTTIES STYLE

Rheingold, Howard. *The Virtual Community.* 1993.
http://www.well.com/user/hlr/vcbook/ (17 Aug. 1996).

SCIENTIFIC STYLE

Rheingold, H. (1993). *The virtual community.*
http://www.well.com/user/hlr/vcbook/ (17 Aug. 1996).

Print publication information should be included if available, followed by the electronic publication information. For example:

HUMANITIES STYLE

Conrad, Joseph. *An Outcast of the Islands.* Garden City, NY:
Doubleday, 1921. Comp. Judy Boss. 1996. *Electronic Text Center at
the University of Virginia.*
http://etext.lib.virginia.edu/etcbin/toccer-new?id=ConOutc&tag
=public&images=images/modeng&data=/texts/english/modeng/
parsed&part=0 (22 Aug. 1996).

SCIENTIFIC STYLE

Conrad, J. (1921/1996). *An outcast of the islands.* Garden City, NY:
Doubleday. (J. Boss, Comp.). *Electronic Text Center at the University
of Virginia.*
http://etext.lib.virginia.edu/etcbin/toccer-new?id=ConOutc&tag=
public&images=images/modeng&data=/texts/english/modeng/
parsed&part=0 (22 Aug. 1996).

Works that have been previously published online may include
original online publication information as well. Some of these
sites are "mirrors," that is, they have copied information published
at another domain. The information at the original site may have
changed, however, without notification to the mirror site. If possible, cite the original source. Other works may be published on a
personal site as well as in an online journal. It is essential to note
which version you are citing as it may constitute a unique edition
of the work or, at any rate, may contain some variations.

2.2.1 Titles

Determining title information for electronic documents and files
is often difficult. Sometimes, too, it is difficult to determine
whether a file is "book length" (if that description any longer
holds meaning) or whether it is part of a larger body of work. A

document may be published in a stand-alone version as well as within a larger work, such as an online journal, and the file may or may not use the same title at both addresses, or one version may change while the other remains static. Graphics, audio, video, and other types of multimedia files may not provide any title information at all. Names given to objects in MOOs and MUDs pose similar dilemmas, as object names and aliases may change at any time although the object number remains the same—at least until the object is recycled.

For academic documents on the WWW, chapter 5 outlines suggestions to help standardize title information (see section 5.12). Authors should follow these guidelines when feasible. One suggestion we have made in this book is to use file names when no title information is available. Other solutions may become apparent as the electronic world continues to evolve.

Titles of online books, journals, and similar works should be italicized. You should also italicize the name of online sites such as MOOs and MUDs and other sites that collect and present the works of multiple authors. For example:

HUMANITIES STYLE

"WWW Utilities (#87)." *DaMOO*. http://damoo.csun.edu:8888/
browse/object/87 (22 Aug. 1996).

SCIENTIFIC STYLE

WWW utilities (#87). *DaMOO*. http://damoo.csun.edu:8888/
browse/object/87 (22 Aug. 1996).

The titles of online databases and information service providers (such as *America Online*) should also be italicized for the same reason. (See chapter 4 for information on how to format titles in files to be submitted to a publisher for print publication.) Italics rather than underlining should be used whenever possible because in hypertext underlining usually represents text that is a link to another document or another section of a document (see chapter 5).

Other electronic documents and files should be cited in the same manner as article titles. In humanities style, the titles of most electronic documents are enclosed in quotation marks:

> Reid, Elizabeth M. "Cultural Formations in Text-Based Virtual Realities." Thesis. U of Melbourne, 1994. http://www.ee.mu.oz.au/papers/emr/cult-form.html (19 Sep. 1996).

In scientific style, titles of articles appear without quotation marks, underlining, or italics, and only the first word of the title and any proper nouns are capitalized.

> Reid, E. M. (1994). Cultural formations in text-based virtual realities. (Master's thesis, U of Melbourne, 1994). http://www.ee.mu.oz.au/papers/emr/cult-form.html (19 Sep. 1996).

It may sometimes be difficult to determine the title of an online file, or files may have more than one title. For example, in figure 2.3 the author has included a title on the page, but the hypertext header lists another title, as shown in the title bar at the top of the browser. (For more information on titles in hypertext documents, see also chapter 5.) For most citation purposes, use the title on the page itself, if available, as provided by the author. For example, the citation for the page in figure 2.3 would read:

HUMANITIES STYLE

> Cressia, Lori L. "Copyright and Fair Use." 1997. http://www.cas.usf.edu/english/walker/courses/fall97/cressiatoc.html (27 Dec. 1997).

SCIENTIFIC STYLE

> Cressia, L. L. (1997). Copyright and fair use.

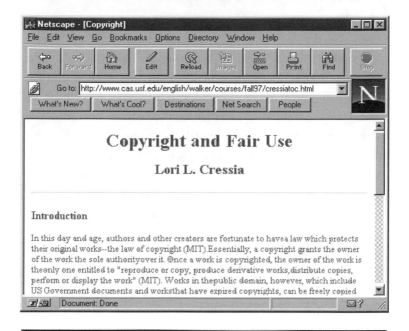

Figure 2.3 A Hypertext Page with Titles and Headers

http://www.cas.usf.edu/english/walker/courses/fall97/cressiatoc. html(27 Dec. 1997).

2.2.2 Place of Publication and Publisher's Name

Traditional citation formats include the city of publication and the publisher's name. This information allows users to locate a given source more easily: if it is not available in the library, we may contact the publisher. We can also be assured we are using the same source as that referenced. Additionally, the name of the press has often been a means of determining the reliability of a given work for academic purposes, with university presses generally considered to be better sources than more popular ones.

For electronic sources, the domain name may also help a reader locate a particular source. If a work is no longer available at a given URL, it may be possible to contact the Web master for the domain and locate the author or file. If the file is located in the same domain as the given URL, we can also be fairly sure we are looking at the same file as that referenced, not a mirror site or some other work with the same title. Domain names may also help somewhat to determine the reliability of an electronic source (see section 2.2.2.1 for more information on domain names). Whether a file is located on an educational server or a commercial server may provide some sense of its reliability. However, as for print sources, the ultimate test of validity is not who published it but the text itself and the critical reading and thinking skills of those who rely on it.

For electronic sources, publication information includes the protocol and address or the name of the information provider, plus any commands or search terms necessary to access the source. The date of access is also included for most electronic sources. In citations of electronic sources published on fixed media, such as CD-ROM, diskettes, or magnetic tape, include the city of publication, the name of the publisher, and any keywords or search path information, if applicable. Citations of sources published on fixed media need not include the date of access.

2.2.2.1 Internet sources

For Internet sources, the first part of the URL designates the protocol. This is followed by the domain name, which indicates the site where the work is published. Thus the URL provides the information necessary to access a source and replaces the usual publication information required in citations of print publications. The URL also furnishes important information to help one ascertain the reliability of a source.

Consider the following URL:

http://www.cas.usf.edu/english/walker/janice.html

Here "http://" designates the protocol (Hypertext Transfer Protocol), and "www.cas.usf.edu" is the domain, in this case the World Wide Web server (www) for the College of Arts and Sciences (cas) at the University of South Florida (usf), an educational institution (edu).

URLs may also contain directories, subdirectories, and file names. In this example, the directory name "english" (Department of English at the University of South Florida) follows the domain name, then the subdirectory, "walker" (the login name of the file owner in this case) appears, and finally the file itself, "janice.html" (a document in Hypertext Markup Language format), is listed. Some URLs may contain additional subdirectories, or file names may be omitted if the file is a default (a file the browser automatically points to in the absence of a file name).

While not all domain names are as easy to translate as this example, they are all registered; it is therefore possible, theoretically at least, to track down the so-called publisher of an "out-of-print" document on the Internet. Figure 2.4 lists some common domain and country extensions.

2.2.2.2 Electronic databases

Electronic publications and software packages will usually list a software publisher or online publisher. This information should be included in the citation in the same manner as for print publications. Search terms (if applicable) should also be included to facilitate access to the specific file or information cited. For example:

HUMANITIES STYLE

Abdul-Ghani, Mohamed. "Comparison of the Effect of Instructional versus Industry-Specific Computer Simulation on Students

Domains		Countries	
.com	commercial	.au	Australia
.gov	government	.ca	Canada
.edu	institutional	.nz	New Zealand
.org	organization	.uk	United Kingdom
.mil	military	.us	United States

Figure 2.4 Common Domain Extensions

Learning in a Front Office Management Course." *DAI* 56 (1996): 4363A. U of Tennessee, 1995. *Dissertation Abstracts Online. OCLC* (22 May 1996).

Kunz, Jennifer, and Stephen J. Bahr. "A Profile of Parental Homicide Against Children." *Journal of Family Violence.* Dec. 1996: 347–364. *Searchbank* +kunz+parental violence (17 Apr. 1997).

SCIENTIFIC STYLE

Abdul-Ghani, M. (1996). Comparison of the effect of instructional versus industry-specific computer simulation on students learning in a front office management course. (Doctoral dissertation, U of Tennessee, 1995). *Dissertation Abstracts International, 56,* 4363A. *Dissertation Abstracts Online. OCLC* (22 May 1996).

Kunz, J., & Bahr, S. J. (1996, December). A profile of parental homicide against children. *Journal of Family Violence,* 347–364. *Searchbank* +kunz+parental violence (17 Apr. 1997).

2.2.3 Publication Medium

An important feature of electronic files is that they are readily transferable from one medium to another: files may be downloaded from their online homes and saved to disks; CD-ROM titles may be installed on a user's hard drive; and most formats may be printed out. For this reason, identifying the publication medium in the bibliographic reference may be meaningless. It certainly violates the principle of economy in that the protocol or publication information is usually sufficient to locate the source. Even designating a specific software publication medium such as CD-ROM is problematic. Some software is available on either diskette or CD-ROM, with no change in the content of the software package itself. There are important differences, however, between one version of the software and the next, thus indicating the version number and date of publication is key to pointing the reader to the specific edition. For example:

HUMANITIES STYLE

WordPerfect Vers. 6.1 for Windows. Orem, UT: Novell, 1994.

Zieger, Herman E. "Aldehyde." *The Software Toolworks Multimedia Encyclopedia*. Vers. 1.5. Boston: Grolier, 1992.

SCIENTIFIC STYLE

WordPerfect Vers. 6.1 for Windows. (1996). Ottawa, ON: Corel.

Zieger, H. E. (1992). Aldehyde. *The software toolworks multimedia encyclopedia* (Version 1.5). Boston: Grolier.

For Internet sources, the protocol (i.e., "http") in a URL designates the medium as online. Information accessed through subscription services such as *America Online, CompuServe,* or *Dissertation Abstracts Online* is also online, although it may only be accessible to fee-paying subscribers.

2.2.4 Publication or Edition Dates

Because many Web sites do not include publication or revision dates, the date of access may be the only way to designate what amounts to the edition of the work in cyberspace. If the author has designated a publication or revision date, this should be included in the citation. In humanities style, place the document date or the date of last revision or modification after the title.

> Throop, David R. "Is a Bad Man Worse than No Man at All?" 25 Sep. 1995. http://www.vix.com/men/nofather/articles/howbad.html (19 Sep. 1996).

In scientific style, the document date, or date of last revision or modification, is enclosed in parentheses and placed after the author's name:

> Throop, D. R. (1995, September 25). Is a bad man worse than no man at all? http://www.vix.com/men/nofather/articles/howbad.html (19 Sep. 1996).

The date the document or file was last accessed is essential to note because an author may have altered a document without changing its dates. The access date, then, identifies the unique edition of the work that a writer has referenced. It is placed in parentheses at the end of the citation, after the Internet address (19 Sep. 1996 in the example above). If the access date and the document date are the same, omit the document date.

2.2.5 Pagination

Some people still believe that a publication of one or two pages is not a reliable source of information for academic works. On the WWW, however, a given source is always one page, regardless of its length. Pagination is thus an element of print publication that has little or no meaning in electronic documents and files. It is handy for locating a specific part of a text, however, and to replace it many software packages offer search or find features. Authors may also choose to embed page anchors, section numbers, or other navigational features within electronic files (see sections

5.5., 5.13, and 5.14 for more information). In the future, it may even be possible for authors to link to specific parts of other works, even those whose authors have not provided the means for doing so.

Screens, printer dependency, monitor capability, and software all affect "page" or "screen" representations. Unless an author has included page numbers in an electronic document, then, it effectively consists of only one page, regardless of its length. In any case, pagination is an artifact of print culture and unnecessary in citations of most electronic sources, which can usually be searched for keywords and phrases using search or find protocols in most word-processing software and Internet browsers, such as *Netscape* and *Microsoft Internet Explorer*. What cannot be omitted, however, is information to allow readers to locate the source, i.e., the URL or other necessary publication information.

DOCUMENTING SOURCES IN THE TEXT

As noted earlier, parenthetical or in-text references to print publications usually include the author's last name and the page number of the reference (humanities style) or the author's last name, the date of publication, and the page number of the reference (scientific style). Following the principle of economy, subsequent references to the same work usually include only a page number, until another in text reference intervenes. For electronic sources, however, unless the author has specifically designated "page" numbers (or other identifiers such as paragraph or section numbers) within the document or file, pagination does not exist. Again, many browsers and programs will allow readers to find the exact location of a reference in a document. Thus, for electronic sources, parenthetical references will usually include only the author's last name (for humanities style) or the author's last name and the date of publication (for scientific style).

2.3 Author's Name

HUMANITIES STYLE

To cite electronic sources within the text, the author's last name is sufficient. For example:

> One fact that cannot be denied is that "We live in an age in which rapid change is certain" (Ambrose).

When the author's name is included in the text, omit the parenthetical reference:

> According to Stephen Ambrose, the real technological revolution began in the nineteenth century, not the twentieth.

SCIENTIFIC STYLE

List the author's last name followed by a comma and the date of publication:

> One fact that cannot be denied is that "We live in an age in which rapid change is certain" (Ambrose, 1996).

When the author's name is mentioned in the text, include the date in parentheses after the author's name:

> According to Stephen Ambrose (1996), the real technological revolution began in the nineteenth century, not the twentieth.

If no publication date is available, use the date accessed, in day-month-year format. For example:

> The "@go" command allows players in MOOs to move instantly between rooms (Bartorillo, 3 Oct. 1996).

When the author's name is included in the text, if no publication date is available, use the access date, in parentheses:

Bartorillo (3 Oct. 1996) says the "@go" command allows players in MOOs to move instantly between rooms.

2.4 Multiple Works by the Same Author

HUMANITIES STYLE

For multiple works by the same author, include the author's last name, followed by a comma and a shortened version of the title, italicized or enclosed in quotation marks as applicable. For example:

> The author is best known, perhaps, for his colorful depictions of life on the Mississippi River and use of dialect: "Whar is you? Dog my cats ef I didn' hear sumf'n," says Jim, the slave (Twain, *Huckleberry Finn*). The use of dialect is evident in other works as well, reaching across the globe and back across the centuries, to King Arthur's Court, using key words and phrases such as "Marry" and "Prithee" to lend credibility to an incredible story (Twain, *Connecticut Yankee*).

Again, if any of this information is mentioned in the text, there is no need to provide it within parentheses as well:

> Mark Twain is best known, perhaps, for his colorful depictions of life on the Mississippi River and use of dialect: "Whar is you? Dog my cats ef I didn' hear sumf'n," says Jim, the slave, in Twain's *Huckleberry Finn*.

In the list of works cited, replace second and subsequent listings of the author's name with three dashes. Alphabetize the works by the first major word of the title.

> Twain, Mark. *The Adventures of Huckleberry Finn*. New York: Harper and Brothers, 1884.
> http://etext.lib.virginia.edu/etcbin/browse-mixed-new?id=Twa2 Huc&tag=public&images=images/modeng&data=/lv1/Archive/ eng-parsed (28 May 1997).

---. *A Connecticut Yankee in King Arthur's Court.* New York: Harper and Brothers, 1889. http://etext.lib.virginia.edu/etcbin/browse-mixed-new?id=Twa Yank&tag=public&images=images/modeng&data=/texts/english/ modeng/parsed (28 May 1997).

SCIENTIFIC STYLE

For multiple works by the same author, include the author's last name followed by a comma and the year of publication.

Technology education has usually approached societal issues from the standpoint of the impact of technology on society (Pannabecker, 1991). However, technology education must help students interpret technological innovations "in the context of technology" (Pannabecker, 1995).

In the list of references, arrange bibliographic entries chronologically, beginning with the earliest year of publication. The author's name is repeated in each entry, rather than being replaced by dashes, as in humanities style:

Pannabecker, J. R. (1991, Fall). Technological impacts and determinism in technology education: Alternate metaphors from social constructivism. *Journal of Technology Education, 3*(1). gopher://borg.lib.vt.edu:70/00/jte/v3n1/pannabecker.jte-v3n1 (29 May 1997).

Pannabecker, J. R. (1995, Fall). For a history of technology education: Contexts, systems, and narratives. *Journal of Technology Education, 7*(1). http://scholar.lib.vt.edu/ejournals/JTE/jte-v7n1/pannabecker. jte-v7n1.html (29 May 1997).

For multiple works by the same author with the same year of publication, designate the publications with lowercase letters directly following the year of publication (i.e., 1990a, 1990b) in both in-text citations and the list of references.

2.5 No Author Listed

HUMANITIES STYLE

For in-text citations when no author is listed, use the document title or a shortened version of the title, enclosed in quotation marks or italicized as appropriate, instead of the author's name:

("Copyright Resources")

SCIENTIFIC STYLE

When no author is listed, use the document title or a shortened version of it (italicizing titles of larger works, if applicable), followed by the document date or the date of access if no document date is given:

(Copyright resources, 25 Sep, 1996)

2.6 Navigation

2.6.1 Section or Paragraph Numbers

List page, section, or paragraph numbers at the conclusion of the citation, separated by commas, if they are included in the original text:

HUMANITIES STYLE

One important reason for the move to electronic writing is that "it is becoming very much cheaper to store information in electronic form and comparatively more expensive to store it as paper" (Goodwin, sec. 1.1).

SCIENTIFIC STYLE

One important reason for the move to electronic writing is that "it is becoming very much cheaper to store information in electronic form and comparatively more expensive to store it as paper" (Goodwin, 1993, sec. 1.1).

If the author's name is cited in the text, list only the page, paragraph, or section number in parentheses at the end of the reference, and, in scientific style, place the year of publication immediately after the author's name:

HUMANITIES STYLE

According to John E. Goodwin, one reason for the move to electronic writing is that it is cheaper (sec. 1.1).

SCIENTIFIC STYLE

According to John E. Goodwin (1993), one reason for the move to electronic writing is that "it is becoming very much cheaper to store information in electronic form" (sec. 1.1).

2.7 Subsequent References to the Same Work

In citations of print sources, subsequent references to the same work need not repeat the author's name, instead giving the different page number or location, if applicable. With electronic documents that are not paginated or otherwise delineated, however, repeating the author's name may be the only way to acknowledge when information is being drawn from a given source. If there are multiple references to the same source within a paragraph, reserve the parenthetical material for the end of the paragraph. Whenever possible, you should incorporate references into the text itself to avoid awkwardness. For a more complete discussion of parenthetical and in-text citations, see the manual for the style you have selected.

PREPARING THE BIBLIOGRAPHIC MATERIAL

When preparing documents for print, the list of works cited (in humanities style) or list of references (in scientific style) should begin on a separate page following the text. (See chapter 4 for information on preparing manuscripts for submission to publishers; see chapter 5 for information on hypertext documents.) In hypertext documents, the list of works cited is often a separate file and may be linked from the table of contents or main page. For printed documents, the pages should be numbered sequentially and double-spaced throughout. Use a hanging indent when listing entries, so that the first line of each entry is flush with the left-hand margin and with the second and subsequent lines of each entry indented five spaces, or one-half inch. Do not use the space bar or tab key to indent lines; instead, use the hanging indent feature in your word processor or otherwise set the left margin so that runover lines are indented automatically. Titles of complete works should be italicized because, as noted earlier, underlining is used to designate hypertextual links in World Wide Web documents. (In many newer word processors and email clients, email addresses and URLs may automatically be formatted as hypertext links through changes in font size or color and the addition of underlining. See chapter 4 for more information on using these programs to create files for print publication.) Entries should be alphabetized by the author's or editor's last name or by the first major word of the title if no author is given.

HUMANITIES STYLE

The basic format for citing electronic sources in humanities style is:

> Author's Last Name, First Name. "Title of Document." *Title of Complete Work* [if applicable]. Version or File Number [if applicable].
> Document date or date of last revision [if different from access date].
> Protocol and address, access path or directories (date of access).

The basic format for citing electronic sources in scientific style is:

Author's Last Name, Initial(s). (Date of document [if different from date accessed]). Title of document. *Title of complete work* [if applicable]. Version or File number [if applicable]. (Edition or revision [if applicable]). Protocol and address, access path, or directories (date of access).

When information is not available, obviously you cannot include it, but give as much as you can. The following examples are grouped according to method of access, or protocol, which is a key element in locating electronic documents and files. For the elements of electronic files, see the specific examples below. For file types not included here, follow the guidelines in the style manual you are using (i.e., MLA, APA, etc.), translating the unique elements of electronic files following the formats presented here.

2.8 The World Wide Web (WWW)

The World Wide Web has made finding information on the Internet quicker and easier and is quickly gaining acceptance as a site for research and publication. Point-and-click browsers such as *Netscape* and *Microsoft Internet Explorer,* powerful online search engines, colorful graphics, real-time audio and video files, and service providers such as *America Online* and *Microsoft Network* offering flat-rate unlimited access accounts have enticed more and more people to search for information sources online, and schools and universities, government agencies, publishers, businesses, and individuals are connecting in record numbers. Like print-based information, information found on the World Wide Web must also be documented, following the same general guidelines as for citing print publications. Sometimes, however, finding the elements included in traditional citation formats is difficult, and sometimes those elements, such as page numbers, may not exist. The following examples follow traditional formats as closely as possible, while acknowledging the unique features of these sources. Again, note that you should insert punctuation exactly as shown.

2.8.1 General Format

HUMANITIES STYLE

To cite files available on the World Wide Web, give the author's name, last name first (if known); the full title of the work, in quotation marks; the title of the complete work (if applicable), in italics; any version or file numbers; and the date of the document or last revision (if available). Next, list the protocol (e.g., "http") and the full URL, followed by the date of access in parentheses.

> Author's Last Name, First Name. "Title of Document or File." *Title of Complete Work or Site.* Version or file number. Date of document. Protocol and address (date of access).

For example:

> Burka, Lauren P. "A Hypertext History of Multi-User Dimensions." *MUD History.* 1993. http://www.utopia.com/talent/lpb/muddex/ essay (2 Aug. 1996).

SCIENTIFIC STYLE

In this style, give the author's last name and initials (if known) and the date of publication in parentheses. Next, list the full title of the work, capitalizing only the first word and any proper nouns; the title of the complete work or site (if applicable) in italics, again capitalizing only the first word and any proper nouns; any version of file numbers, enclosed in parentheses; the protocol and address, including the path or directories necessary to access the document; and finally the date accessed, enclosed in parentheses.

> Author's Last Name, Initial(s). (Document date). Title of document. *Title of complete work* (Version or file number[s]). Protocol and address (date of access).

For example:

> Burka, L. P. (1993). A hypertext history of multi-user dimensions. *MUD history.* http://www.utopia.com/talent/lpb/muddex/essay (2 Aug. 1996).

2.8.2 A Revision

HUMANITIES STYLE

Include the date of the last revision preceded by the abbreviation "Rev." or the date of last modification preceded by the abbreviation "Mod." before the URL:

> Walker, Janice R. "MLA-Style Citations of Electronic Sources." Rev. Apr. 1995. http://www.cas.usf.edu/english/walker/mla.html (10 May 1996).

SCIENTIFIC STYLE

In parentheses after the title, include the date of last revision preceded by the abbreviation "Rev." or the date of last modification preceded by the abbreviation "Mod.":

> Walker, J. R. (1995). MLA-style citations of electronic sources (Rev. Apr. 1995). http://www.cas.usf.edu/english/walker/mla.html (10 May 1996).

2.8.3 A Version Other than the First

HUMANITIES STYLE

Preceded by the abbreviation "Vers.," insert the version number immediately following the title and before any revision or modification information. Generally, if the version or edition is the first, the version number is omitted from the citation.

Tilton, James "Eric." "Composing Good HTML." Vers. 2.0.5. Mod. 8 Dec. 1995. http://www.cs.cmu.edu/~tilt/cgh/ (5 Aug. 1995).

SCIENTIFIC STYLE

Preceded by the word "Version," include the version number in parentheses immediately following the title and before any revision or modification dates. As in humanities style, if the version or edition is the first, you may omit this information from the citation.

Tilton, J. (1995). Composing good HTML (Version 2.0.5). (Mod. 8 Dec. 1995). http://www.cs.cmu.edu/~tilt/cgh/ (5 Aug. 1995).

2.8.4 No Individual Author Listed

Sometimes no individual author is listed for a site. In this case, use the name of the news service, group or organization, corporation, or government agency, if applicable, in place of the author's name.

2.8.4.1 An article from a news service

HUMANITIES STYLE

Give the name of the news service; the title of the article, enclosed in quotation marks; the title of the site or online newspaper (if applicable), in italics; and the date of publication (if applicable). Next, list the protocol and address, followed by the date accessed, in parentheses.

Associated Press. "Scientists Capture Gene that Makes Worms Live Longer." *The Globe Online* 7 Aug. 1996. http://www.globe.com/globe/ap/cgi-bin/retrieve.cgi?/globe/apwir /220/nat/aa066707 (23 Sep. 1996).

SCIENTIFIC STYLE

Include the name of the news service, followed by the date of publication (if different from the access date) in parentheses, the title of the article, the title of the online news service (if applicable) in italics, and the protocol and address. Conclude with the date accessed in parentheses.

> Associated Press. (1996, August 7). Scientists capture gene that makes worms live longer. *The Globe Online.* http://www.globe.com/globe/ap/cgi-bin/retrieve.cgi?/globe/apwir/ 220/nat/aa066707 (14 Aug. 1996).

2.8.4.2 A Work by a group or organization

HUMANITIES STYLE

Include the name of the group or organization as the author. Continue with the title of the file, enclosed in quotation marks; the title of the complete work (if applicable), in italics; any version or file numbers; the date of publication (if known); and the protocol and address, followed by the date accessed, in parentheses. If the title of the site is the same as the group or organization name, it is not necessary to repeat it.

> Purdue University On-Line Writing Lab. "Writing Research Papers: A Step-by-Step Procedure." 1995. http://owl.trc.purdue.edu/Files/94.html (7 Aug. 1996).

SCIENTIFIC STYLE

Include the name of the group or organization, followed by the document date in parentheses if different from the date accessed. Next, list the title of the article, the title of the complete work (if applicable) in italics, the protocol and address, and the date accessed, in parentheses.

Coalition to Prevent the Destruction of Canada Geese. (1996).
Canada geese as a suburban wildlife issue (Mod. 7 Jun. 1997).
http://www.icu.com/geese/doc3.html (12 Jun. 1997).

2.8.4.3 Corporate home pages and information

HUMANITIES STYLE

Give the name of the corporation; the title of the page, enclosed in
quotation marks; the title of the complete site (if applicable and if
different from the name of the corporate author), in italics; the
date of publication (if applicable); and then the protocol and address, followed by the date accessed in parentheses.

Corel Corporation. "Welcome to Corel—Visitor Center." 29 May
1996. http://www corel.com/Aboutcorel/ (8 Aug. 1996).

SCIENTIFIC STYLE

List the name of the corporation, the date of publication (if different from the date accessed) in parentheses, the title of the page,
the title of the complete site (if applicable and if different from the
name of the corporate author) in italics, the protocol and address,
and the date accessed, also enclosed in parentheses.

Corel Corporation. (1996, May 29). Welcome to Corel—Visitor
center. http://www.corel.com/Aboutcorel/ (8 Aug. 1996).

2.8.4.4 Government information and sites

HUMANITIES STYLE

List the name of the government agency; the title of the site, enclosed in quotation marks; any version or file numbers (if applicable); the date of publication or last revision (if applicable); and
the protocol and address, followed by the date accessed, in parentheses.

U.S. Patent and Trademark Office. "Intellectual Property and the National Infrastructure: The Report of the Working Group on Intellectual Property Rights." 1995. http://www.uspto.gov:80/web/offices/com/doc/ipnii/ipnii.txt (30 Dec. 1997).

SCIENTIFIC STYLE

List the name of the government agency followed by the document date in parentheses (if different from the date accessed), the title of the document or site, any file or version numbers in parentheses, the protocol and address, and the date accessed in parentheses.

U.S. Department of Commerce. (1997, December). Transmittal form (PTO/SB/21). http://www.uspto.gov:80/web/forms/sb0021.pdf (15 Dec. 1997).

2.8.5 Maintained Sites

Some sites are maintained rather than authored by an individual or group. The site may contain information from various sources or may index other sites.

The name of the site maintainer or Web master will usually be listed after the title of the page or site. However, the placement of the name will depend on whether you are referencing the site itself or the work of the maintainer.

2.8.5.1 Referencing the site

HUMANITIES STYLE

List the author's name (if applicable); the title of the page or site, enclosed in quotation marks or italicized as appropriate; and the abbreviation "Maint." (for "Maintained by") followed by the name of the site maintainer or Web master. Next, list the date of publication or last revision (if applicable), the protocol and address, and the date of access, in parentheses.

"The Contemporary European Studies Association of Australia."
Maint. Robert R. Wagner. 8 Aug. 1996.
http://www.arts.unimelb.edu.au/projects/cesaa/index.html (9 Aug.
1996).

SCIENTIFIC STYLE

List the author's name (if applicable); the date of publication or
last revision, in parentheses; and the title of the page. If no author
is listed, begin with the title of the page, followed by the date of
publication, in parentheses. Next, list the name of the site's maintainer, followed by the abbreviation "Maint.," in parentheses, and
the usual publication information. Close with the date of access,
in parentheses.

The contemporary European studies association of Australia. (1996,
August 8). (R. R. Wagner, Maint.).
http://www.arts.unimelb.edu.au/projects/cesaa/index.html (9 Aug.
1996).

2.8.5.2 Referencing the maintainer

HUMANITIES STYLE

If your focus is on the work of the maintainer, then list the name
of the site maintainer, last name first, followed by the abbreviation
"maint." and the usual citation information.

Wagner, Robert R., maint. "The Contemporary European Studies
Association of Australia." 8 Aug. 1996.
http://www.arts.unimelb.edu.au/projects/cesaa/index.html (9 Aug.
1996).

SCIENTIFIC STYLE

In references to the work of the site maintainer, list the last name
and initials of the site maintainer followed by the abbreviation
"Maint." in parentheses and the usual citation information.

Wagner, R. R. (Maint.). (1996, August 8). The contemporary
European studies association of Australia.
http://www.arts.unimelb.edu.au/projects/cesaa/index.html (9 Aug.
1996).

2.8.6 Compiled Sites

On the WWW, sometimes a site is a compilation of links rather
than a singly authored document or file, that is, an individual has
gathered conversations or files from other sources to create a collaborative work. The placement of the compiler's name depends
on the focus of your reference.

2.8.6.1 Referencing the site

HUMANITIES STYLE

List the author's name if applicable, the title of the page, the complete title of the site (if applicable), and then the abbreviation
"Comp." and the name of the compiler. Continue with the standard publication information.

> "Electronic Feedback: *CMC Magazine* Visits the Netoric Cafe." Comp.
> Mick Doherty. *Computer Mediated Communication Magazine* 2.3
> (1995): 41. http://sunsite.unc.edu/cmc/mag/1995/mar/netoric.html
> (10 Aug. 1996).

SCIENTIFIC STYLE

List the author's name (if applicable) and, in parentheses, the date
of publication. For works with no author, begin with the title of
the page followed by the date of publication in parentheses. Next,
list the name of the compiler and the abbreviation "Comp." enclosed in parentheses. Conclude with the standard publication information.

> Office systems curriculum and careers. (1997). (M. Valenti, Comp.).
> http://www.geocities.com/CollegePark/3421/ (30 Dec. 1997).

2.8.6.2 Referencing the compiler

HUMANITIES STYLE

List the last name of the compiler, the first name, and the abbreviation "comp." Follow with the usual citation information.

> Doherty, Mick, comp. "Electronic Feedback: *CMC Magazine* Visits the Netoric Cafe." *Computer Mediated Communication Magazine* 2.3 (1995): 41. http://sunsite.unc.edu/cmc/mag/1995/mar/netoric.html (10 Aug. 1996).

SCIENTIFIC STYLE

List the last name and initials of the compiler, the abbreviation "Comp." in parentheses, the document date or date of last revision (if applicable) in parentheses, and the usual publication information.

> Valenti, M. (Comp.). (1997). Office systems curriculum and careers. http://www.geocities.com/CollegePark/3421/ (30 Dec. 1997).

2.8.7 No Author Listed

HUMANITIES STYLE

To cite a document or file with no author or organization listed, begin with the title of the page, enclosed in quotation marks, and then list the title of the complete site (if applicable), in italics; the document date (if different from the date accessed); the protocol and address; and, enclosed in parentheses, the date accessed.

> "Web Gateway Page." *Diversity University Main Campus MOO.* http://128.18.101.106:8888/ (7 Sep. 1996).

SCIENTIFIC STYLE

Begin with the title of the page, with only the first word and any proper nouns capitalized, followed by the publication date (if different from the date accessed), enclosed in parentheses, and the usual publication information.

> A clue on brain functioning. (1997, August 11). *The Inquirer.*
> http://www.phillynews.com/inquirer/97/Aug/11/health_and_
> sciences/WHAT11.htm (30 Dec. 1997).

2.8.8 No Author or Title Listed

HUMANITIES STYLE

To cite a document or file with no discernible author or title, include the file name and the document date (if known and if different from the date accessed), followed by the usual publication information.

> 1993e-small.gif. http://encke.jpl.nasa.gov/images/1993e-small.gif (27
> May 1997).

SCIENTIFIC STYLE

Include the file name, followed by the type of file (if applicable) enclosed in square brackets, the document date (if known and if different from the date accessed) enclosed in parentheses, and the usual publication information.

> hexpal2.jpg. [graphics file]. (1996).
> http://www.cas.usf.edu/english/walker/pix/hexpal2.jpg (30Dec.
> 1997).

2.8.9 Documents with Frames

Documents published in frames do not always indicate unique URLs for each page. List the URL for the main page, and show the links followed to access the specific page or file being cited. If the file is available in a nonframe version or if your browser provides site information on documents contained in frames, you may choose to cite the unique URL for the file being cited rather than that for the main site.

HUMANITIES STYLE

To cite a WWW file in frames, list the author's name (if available), last name first; the title of the document or file, enclosed in quotation marks; the version or file number (if applicable); the document date (if applicable and if different from the date accessed); the full title of the site (if applicable), in italics; and the usual publication information, including the path or links followed to access the specific frame, separated from the URL by a single blank space.

> Haile, Mitchell. "Research and Reference Starting Links." Vers. 2.0.
> Rev. 22 Jun. 1996. *Internet Starting Links.* Vers. 2.1b6.
> http://www.nyx.net/~jhaile/ Research and Reference (3 Aug. 1996).

SCIENTIFIC STYLE

List the author's last name and initials (if known); the date of the document or file (if available and if different from the date accessed), in parentheses; the title of the document and (if applicable) the version or file number, in parentheses; the title of the complete work, in italics; the usual publication information, including the path or links followed to access the specific frame, separated from the URL by a single blank space; and the date accessed, enclosed in parentheses.

> Haile, M. (1996, June 22). Research and reference starting links
> (Vers. 2.0). *Internet starting links* (Vers. 2.1b6). http://www.nyx.
> net/~jhaile/ Research and Reference (3 Aug. 1996).

2.8.10 Citing a Link from a WWW Document

HUMANITIES STYLE

To cite a file as a link from another site, give the name of the author of the linked file (if known); the title of the link, enclosed in quotation marks; and the publication date (if applicable and if different from the date accessed). Next, give the title of the site containing the link (if applicable), enclosed in quotation marks and preceded by "Lkd. in," and continue with the usual publication information, including the path or links followed to access the specific file, separated from the URL by a single blank space, and concluding with the date of access, enclosed in parentheses.

> Nellen, Ted. "You Are Terrified of Your Own Children." 21 May 1996. Lkd. in "Declaration of Independence for Cyberspace." By John Perry Barlow. *RhetNet*. Vers. 3.13. Rev. 26 Jul. 1996. http://www.missouri.edu/~rhetnet/ snapshots/Declaration of Independence for Cyberspace/You are terrified of your own children (3 Aug. 1996).

SCIENTIFIC STYLE

To cite a file as a link, give the last name and initials of the author; the date of publication if different from the date accessed, in parentheses; and the title of the linked file (if applicable). Next, list the abbreviation "Lkd. in" followed by the name of the author of the site containing the link and the title of the site. Conclude with the usual publication information, including the path or links followed to access the file, separated from the URL by a single blank space, and the date accessed, in parentheses.

> Nellen, T. (1996, May 21). You are terrified of your own children. Lkd. in J. P. Barlow, Declaration of independence in cyberspace. *RhetNet* (9 Feb. 1996). http://www.missouri.edu/~rhetnet/ snapshots/Declaration of Independence for Cyberspace/You are terrified of your own children (3 Aug. 1996).

2.8.11 Citing Anchors in a WWW Page

Some WWW pages include links, called anchors, usually denoted by a pound sign (#) and text after the file name in the URL, which may be used to designate a specific location in a text.

2.8.11.1 With specific note references

When citing a specific note reference in a WWW document, include the exact location of the reference within the document.

HUMANITIES STYLE

To reference a specific portion of a text designated with a named anchor, list the author's name (if known); the title of the specific section being referenced (if applicable), enclosed in quotation marks; the title of the complete site (if applicable), in italics; the date of the article or other edition information; the URL and the pound sign (#) and text following the file name that links to that section; and the date of access, enclosed in parentheses.

> NCSA. "Links to Specific Sections." *A Beginner's Guide to HTML.*
> April 1996. http://www.ncsa.uiuc.edu/General/Internet/WWW/
> HTMLPrimerAll.html#LTS (15 Dec. 1997).

SCIENTIFIC STYLE

Include the author's name (if known), followed by the date of the article or document; the title of the specific section being referenced (if applicable); and the title of the full site (if applicable), in italics. Next, list the URL, followed immediately by the pound sign (#) and text following the file name that links to that section. Conclude the reference with the date accessed in parentheses.

> NCSA. (1996, April). Links to specific sections. *A beginner's guide to*
> *HTML.* http://www.ncsa.uiuc.edu/General/Internet/WWW/HTML
> PrimerAll.html#LTS (15 Dec. 1997).

2.8.11.2 Without specific note references

To cite a specific section of a text as a link, list the URL for the entire document, followed by a single blank space and the linked text.

List the author's name (if applicable); the title of the article, enclosed in quotation marks; and/or the title of the complete site, in italics; the publication date or edition information; the protocol and address; a single blank space and the links or path followed to the referenced section; and the date of access, enclosed in parentheses.

> NCSA. *A Beginner's Guide to HTML.* April 1996.
> http://www.ncsa.uiuc.edu/General/Internet/WWW/HTML
> PrimerAll.html Links to Specific Sections (15 Dec. 1997).

SCIENTIFIC STYLE

List the author's name (if applicable); the date of publication (if known and if different from the date accessed), enclosed in parentheses; the title of the file and/or the title of the complete site, in italics; the protocol and address; a single blank space, followed by the links or path followed to the referenced section; and the date of access, enclosed in parentheses.

> NCSA. (1996, April). *A beginner's guide to HTML.*
> http://www.ncsa.uiuc.edu/General/Internet/WWW/HTML
> PrimerAll.html Links to Specific Sections (15 Dec. 1997).

2.8.12 Citing an Article in an Online Journal

HUMANITIES STYLE

List the author's name, last name first; the title of the article, enclosed in quotation marks; the title of the journal, in italics; and the volume number, followed by a colon and the issue number (if applicable). Place the date of publication in parentheses afer the issue number, and then cite the URL for the journal and the date of access, in parentheses.

Blais, Ellen. "O Brave New Net!" *Computer Mediated Communication Magazine* 3.8 (1996). http://www.december.com/cmc/mag/1996/aug/toc.html (5 Aug. 1996).

SCIENTIFIC STYLE

List the author's last name and initials; the date of publication, enclosed in parentheses; the title of the article; the title of the journal, in italics and followed by a comma; and the volume number of the journal, also in italics. Next, list the issue number, enclosed in parentheses, and the protocol and address of the journal, followed by the date of access, enclosed in parentheses.

Blais, E. (1996). O brave new Net! *Computer Mediated Communication Magazine, 3*(8). http://www.december.com/cmc/ mag/1996/aug/toc.html (5 Aug. 1996).

2.8.12.1 Articles not listed by title or author on main page of journal

Some articles in online journals may not be listed by title or author on the contents page. In such cases, you will need to include the search path or directories you followed to access the article.

HUMANITIES STYLE

After listing the URL and a single blank space, include the search path or directories followed to access the article. Separate directories or paths by a forward slash (/). Conclude with the date of access, enclosed in parentheses.

Ferganchick-Neufang, Julia. K. "Harassment On-Line: Considerations for Women and Webbed Pedagogy." *Kairos* 2.2 (1997). http:// english.ttu.edu/kairos/2.2/index.html CoverWeb/Gender and Electronic Discourse/Harassment On-Line (15 Dec. 1997).

List the search path or directories followed to access the article after the URL, separated by a single blank space. Separate directories or paths by a forward slash (/), and conclude with the date of access, enclosed in parentheses.

> Ferganchick-Neufang, J. K. (1997). Harassment on-line: Considerations for women and Webbed pedagogy. *Kairos, 2*(2). http://english.ttu.edu/kairos/2.2/index.html CoverWeb/Gender and Electronic Discourse/Harassment On-Line (15 Dec. 1997).

2.8.12.2 Citing an article with a unique URL

Some articles may be accessed directly using a unique URL. Include publication information on the journal as well, if known.

HUMANITIES STYLE

> Weisser, Christian R., and Janice R. Walker. "Electronic Theses and Dissertations: Digitizing Scholarship for Its Own Sake." *Journal of Electronic Publishing* 3.2 (1997). http://www.press.umich.edu/jep/03-02/etd.html (15 Dec. 1997).

SCIENTIFIC STYLE

> Weisser, C. R., & Walker, J. R. (1997). Electronic theses and dissertations: Digitizing scholarship for its own sake. *Journal of Electronic Publishing, 3*(2). http://www.press.umich.edu/jep/03-02/etd.html (15 Dec. 1997).

2.8.12.3 A journal article accessed through an archive

If the archive returns a unique URL (that is, if the file can be accessed directly), list it as you normally would for an online journal article (see section 2.8.12, above). Otherwise, include the search path or links followed from the main page (see section 2.8.12.1).

2.8.13 Previously Published Files and Documents

HUMANITIES STYLE

List the author's name; the title of the article (if applicable), enclosed in quotation marks; the original publication information; the title of the archive site; the protocol and address, including any paths or directory commands; and the date of access, in parentheses.

> Giroux, Henry A. "Slacking Off: Border Youth and Postmodern Education." *Journal of Advanced Composition* 14 (1994): 347–66. *JAC Online.* http://www.cas.usf.edu/JAC/jac.html Back Issues/14.2/giroux.html (1 Jan. 1998).

SCIENTIFIC STYLE

List the author's name and initials, followed by the date of publication, in parentheses, the title of the article, and the print publication information (if known). Next, list the title of the archive site (if applicable); the protocol and address for the document, including any paths or directories; and the date accessed, in parentheses.

> Giroux, H. A. (1994). Slacking off: Border youth and postmodern education. *Journal of Advanced Composition, 14*(2), 347–366. *JAC Online.* http://www.cas.usf.edu/JAC/jac.html Back Issues/14.2/giroux.html (1 Jan. 1998).

2.8.14 Citing Graphic, Audio, and Video Files

It is just as important to cite graphic, audio, and video files as it is to cite text files. However, it may be even more difficult to locate the necessary information, such as the name of the artist, composer, or director or the file's URL. The form of your citation will depend on whether your reference is to the graphic, audio, or video itself or to the page on which the graphic, audio, or video file is published. It will also depend on what information about the file you are able to determine.

2.8.14.1 Citing graphic, audio, or video files on the page

HUMANITIES STYLE

If your reference is to a graphic, audio, or video file in the context of the WWW page on which it is published, then cite the name of the artist, composer, or producer (if known), the title of the piece (if known), enclosed in quotation marks or italicized, as applicable, or the name of the file if no title is available. Next, list the date of creation or last modification of the file (if known) and follow with the information for the WWW page on which the file is published.

> Leyster, Judith. *The Concert.* c. 1633. "Permanent Collection Gallery: 17th Century." *National Museum of Women in the Arts.*
> http://www.nmwa.org/legacy/gallery/g1600s1.htm (18 Dec. 1997).

SCIENTIFIC STYLE

Cite the name of the artist, composer, or director (in the case of video files, you may wish to cite the producer as well), if known; the title of the piece or the name of the file; the type of file (i.e., "graphic file," "audio file," or "video file") in square brackets; the date of creation (if known), in parentheses; the title of the page on which it is published, preceded by the name of the author (if applicable); and the protocol and address of the page, followed by the date accessed, in parentheses.

> 1027.me.06.ram [audio file]. Saving Latin American wilderness. *NPR.*
> http://www.npr.org/news/world/costarica (19 Dec. 1997).

> canoe.gif [graphic file]. Saving Latin American wilderness. *NPR.*
> http://www.npr.org/news/world/costarica (19 Dec. 1997).

2.8.14.2 Citing graphic, audio, or video files

HUMANITIES STYLE

If your reference is to the file itself, include the name of the artist, composer, or author, if known (for video files, you may wish to cite the name of the producer as well, if known); the title of the work, enclosed in quotation marks, or the name of the file, not enclosed in quotation marks; publication information (if available); the publication date or date of last modification (if known); the protocol and address; and, in parentheses, the date accessed. Obviously, you may omit any information that is unavailable.

971027.me.06.ram. *Morning Edition.* National Public Radio. 27 Oct. 1997. http://www.npr.org/ramfiles/971027.me.06.ram (19 Dec. 1997).

SCIENTIFIC STYLE

To reference the file itself, include the name of the artist, composer, or author (for video files, include the name of the producer as well), if known; the title of the piece, in italics or enclosed in quotation marks as applicable, or the name of the file if no title is available, followed by the type of file enclosed in square brackets; the date of the piece (if known) in parentheses and followed by a period; any publication information (if available); the unique URL for the file; and the date of access, enclosed in parentheses.

971027.me.06.ram [audio file]. (1997, October 27). *Morning edition* National Public Radio. http://www.npr.org/ramfiles/971027. me.06.ram (19 Dec. 1997).

2.8.15 Citing Document Information Screens

Some browsers will give information on WWW documents that may not be published on the page itself. To cite document information screens, list the information for the page, but with the addition of the words "document information" after the author's name or, if no author is listed, after the title.

HUMANITIES STYLE

> Nelson, Theodor Holm. Document information. "Transcopyright: Pre-Permission for Virtual Publishing." 1995.
> http://www.world3.com/meme1/nelson2.html (8 Aug. 1996).

SCIENTIFIC STYLE

> Nelson, T. H. [document information]. (1995). Transcopyright: Pre-permission for virtual publishing.
> http://www.world3.com/meme1/nelson2.html (8 Aug. 1996).

2.8.16 Citing Document Source Code

HUMANITIES STYLE

Cite the document page or file as you would normally, but include the words "Source code" after the author's name or, if no author is listed, after the title of the page.

> Hughes, Kevin. Source code. "Entering the World-Wide Web: A Guide to Cyberspace." Vers. 6.1.1. 1994.
> http://www.eit.com/web/www.guide/ (8 Aug. 1996).

SCIENTIFIC STYLE

Cite the document page or file as you would normally, but include the words "source code" in square brackets after the author's name or, if no author is listed, after the title of the page.

> Hughes, K. [source code]. (1994). Entering the World-Wide Web: A guide to cyberspace (Version 6.1.1).
> http://www.eit.com/web/www.guide/ (8 Aug. 1996).

2.8.17 Additional Information

Many browsers and client programs used to access the World Wide Web contain information of their own that may be important. For instance, some WWW documents and files refer specifically to the browser software or program necessary to access them adequately. A site may stipulate, for example, "Best Viewed with Netscape 2.0" or "JAVA Enhanced" or "Apple QuickTime Movies." For most multimedia files, the file extension in the Internet address or file name (such as .mov for video files) will be enough; however, include whatever information is necessary to aid the reader in finding the source and to give sufficient credit to your sources. Because these are software programs, see section 2.16, on software programs and video games, for more information.

2.9 Email, Discussion Lists, and Newsgroups

Electronic mail (email), electronic discussion lists, and Bitnet and Usenet newsgroups all follow similar formats, in essence, that of the interoffice memorandum, with a line for the addressee, the author, the date of the message, and a subject line. They may also include information regarding "carbon copies" or additional addresses where the message has been sent, as well as other pertinent information useful to online readers. Electronic mail messages are often brief, and many are personal messages between users, but a number are posted to large discussion groups and may contain valuable information. Traditionally, personal letters are not cited in most bibliographic formats; however, the nature of many public electronic mailing lists constitutes publication, and they should therefore be cited. Even personal messages may sometimes be considered published; however, personal email addresses should be omitted from bibliographic references, and you may wish to request permission from the author to cite the message.

2.9.1 General Format

HUMANITIES STYLE

Cite the author's name (if known) or the author's email or login name (the part of the email address before the @ sign), followed by the subject line of the posting, enclosed in quotation marks; the date of the message if different from the date accessed; and the name of the discussion list (if applicable), in italics. Next, give the address of the list, or the protocol and address of the newsgroup, followed by the date accessed, in parentheses.

> Author's Last Name, First Name or alias. "Subject Line." Message date if different from date accessed. *List Name* [if applicable]. List or newsgroup address (date accessed).

For example:

> Crump, Eric. "Re: Preserving Writing." *Alliance for Computers and Writing Listserv.* acw-l@unicorn.acs.ttu.edu (31 Mar. 1995).

SCIENTIFIC STYLE

Include the author's last name and initials (if known) or the author's alias; the date of the message in parentheses, if different from the date accessed; and the subject line, only first word and proper nouns capitalized. For discussion lists and newsgroups, include the name of the list (if applicable), capitalized as just described and italicized; the list address; and the date accessed, in parentheses.

> Author's Last Name, Initial(s). (Message date). Subject line from message. *List name.* List address or protocol and address (date accessed).

For example:

> Crump, E. Re: Preserving writing. *Alliance for Computers and Writing listserv.* acw-l@unicorn.acs.ttu.edu (31 Mar. 1995).

2.9.2 Messages to Electronic Discussion Lists (Listservs, Listprocs, and Majordomo)

HUMANITIES STYLE

Give the author's name (if known) or alias; the subject line from the posting, in quotation marks; the date of the message if different from the date accessed; the name of the list (if applicable), in italics; the address of the list; and the date accessed, in parentheses.

> Bruckman, Amy S. "MOOSE Crossing Proposal." mediamoo
> @media.mit.edu (20 Dec. 1994).

SCIENTIFIC STYLE

Give the author's name (or alias); the message date if different from the date accessed; the subject line from the posting; the list name (if applicable), in italics; the list address; and the access date, in parentheses.

> Larson, P. M. (1995, October 10). Reply: Impact of the slave trade on
> Africa. h-africa@msu.edu (12 Oct. 1995).

2.9.3 Messages to Newsgroups (Internet and Bulletin Board Services)

HUMANITIES STYLE

Give the author's name (if known) or alias; the subject line from the message, enclosed in quotation marks; and the date of the message if different from the date accessed. Then list the name of the newsgroup (if applicable), in italics, and the protocol and address of the newsgroup, followed by the date accessed, in parentheses.

> Reuters. "Race-based Texas Districts Redrawn." 6 Aug. 1996.
> news.clari.news.issues (9 Aug. 1996).

SCIENTIFIC STYLE

Give the author's name (or alias), the date of message if different from the date accessed, the subject line of message, the name of the newsgroup (if applicable), in italics, the protocol and address of newsgroup, and the date accessed, in parentheses.

> Reuters. (1996, August 6). Race-based Texas districts redrawn. news:clari.news.issues (9 Aug. 1996).

2.9.4 Personal Email Messages (Internet, BBS, and Local Area Networks)

For personal email listings, omit the email address and instead use the words "Personal email."

HUMANITIES STYLE

> Thomson, Barry. "Virtual Reality." Personal email (25 Jan. 1995).

SCIENTIFIC STYLE

In scientific style, personal email is not usually included in the list of references. If included, however, omit the email address and instead insert the words "personal email" in square brackets after the subject line.

> Thomson, B. Virtual reality. [personal email]. (25 Jan. 1995).

2.9.5 BBS or Network Forums and Discussion Groups

Postings to BBS or local network forums should be treated similarly to Internet messages, except that the name of the BBS or network (the company name for business LANs) should be included, in italics, after the subject line of the message. Cite the paths or directories followed to access the forum, if applicable.

HUMANITIES STYLE

BLACK SHP. "THE COTTONWOOD." 25 Jul. 1996. *America Online.* Learning and Culture/The Arts/Independent and Foreign Film/i_LINE:indiefilm online/U Review (12 Aug. 1996).

Hardy, Donald D. "Democratic Webs." *Institute for Workplace Health and Safety.* WWW Forum (12 Nov. 1995).

Sedrag, Ekim. "American Impressionism." 8 Aug. 1996. *Prodigy.* Arts BB/Arts Cafe (12 Aug. 1996).

SCIENTIFIC STYLE

BLACK SHP. (1996, July 25). The Cottonwood. *America Online.* Learning and Culture/The Arts/Independent and Foreign Film/i_LINE:indiefilm online/U Review (12 Aug. 1996).

Hardy, D. D. Democratic webs. *Institute for Workplace Health and Safety.* WWW Forum (12 Nov. 1995).

Sedrag, E. (1996, August 8). American impressionism. *Prodigy.* Arts BB/Arts Cafe (12 Aug. 1996).

2.9.6 Archives

Archives are online repositories that store messages from some electronic lists. If a message is available through an online archive, include the archive name and address in your citation, including any necessary commands to access the message.

2.9.6.1 WWW archives

HUMANITIES STYLE

List the original publication information (if known), followed by the title of the archive site (if applicable), in italics; its address; and the date of access, in parentheses.

Carbone, Nick. "NN960126: Follow-up to Don's Comments about Citing URLs." 26 Jan. 1996. *Alliance for Computers and Writing Listserv.* acw-l@ttacs6.ttu.edu. *Texas Tech University Email Archive for List ACW-L.* http://www.ttu.edu/lists/acw-l 9601 (17 Feb. 1996).

SCIENTIFIC STYLE

Follow the original online publication information (if known) with the title of the archive site (if applicable), in italics; the protocol and address, including any paths or directories; and the date accessed, in parentheses.

Carbone, N. (1996, January 26). NN960126: Follow-up to Don's comments about citing URLs. *Alliance for Computers and Writing listserv.* acw-l@ttacs6.ttu.edu. *Texas Tech University email archive for list ACW-L.* http://www.ttu.edu/lists/acw-l 9601 (17 Feb. 1996).

2.9.6.2 Newsgroup archives

HUMANITIES STYLE

Give the original online publication information (if known) and then the title of the archive site (if applicable), in italics; the protocol and address of the archive site; and the access date, in parentheses.

Danush, Mark. "Backgammon—Frequently Asked Questions." 14 Mar. 1996. news:rec.games.backgammon. ftp://rtfm.mit.edu/pub/usenet-by-group/rec.games.backgammon/ Backgammon_-_Frequently_Asked_Questions._%5Bmonthly %5D (9 Aug. 1996).

SCIENTIFIC STYLE

Follow the usual publication information with the title of the archive site if applicable) in italics; the protocol and address of the archive site; and the date of access, in parentheses.

Danush, M. (1996, March 14). Backgammon—Frequently asked questions. news:rec.games.backgammon. ftp://rtfm.mit.edu/pub/usenet-by-group/rec.games.backgammon/ Backgammon_-_Frequently_Asked_Questions._%5Bmonthly %5D (9 Aug. 1996).

2.9.6.3 Email archives

Some archive sites make files available on request. Often these sites are automated, that is, specific commands are submitted by email and recognized and responded to by a software program. To cite archived messages or files available from these sites, include the email address of the archive and the commmands necessary to access the file.

HUMANITIES STYLE

Vavra, Linda. "H-Rhetor Job List 3/1/96." 29 Feb. 1996. h-rhetor @msu.edu. listserv@msu.edu get h-rhetor log 9602e (1 Jan. 1998).

SCIENTIFIC STYLE

Vavra, L. (1996, February 29). H-Rhetor job list 3/1/96. h-rhetor @msu.edu. listserv@msu.edu get h-rhetor log 9602e (1 Jan. 1998).

2.10 Information Available Using Gopher Protocols

Gopher is a menu-driven protocol for finding information on the Internet. Like telnet, most gopher sites can be accessed using Web browsers, as well as using various gopher client programs. Most gopher sites allow users to read files online, email them, or download them to their personal computers. Gopher sites are usually set up with directories similar to those on your personal computer. When translated into browser URLs, however, gopher directories can be extremely unwieldy. For extremely long directory paths, therefore, you may cite the path in terms of links from the main page rather than listing a unique URL for the file; for electronic documents, however, the unique URL is preferable. Give as much information as necessary to allow readers to locate the source.

2.10.1 General Format

HUMANITIES STYLE

List the author's name (if known), last name first; the title of the paper or file, enclosed in quotation marks; the title of the complete work (if applicable), in italics; and the date of publication (if known), including any previous publication information (if applicable). Include the protocol (i.e., "gopher"), the address, the gopher search path or directories followed to access the information (if applicable), and, in parentheses, the date the file was accessed (if applicable).

> Author's Last Name, First Name. "Title of Work." *Title of Complete Work.* Date of document. Protocol and address, path or directories (date of access).

For example, for files accessed using a Web browser, a citation using the unique URL for the actual file might read:

> African National Congress. "Human Rights Update for Week No. 10 from 5/3/96 to 11/3/97." gopher://gopher.anc.org.za:70/00/hrc/1997/hrup97.10 (1 Jan. 1998).

Pointing to the address of the main page and indicating the links that were followed to access the document, however, the citation becomes:

African National Congress. "Human Rights Update for Week No. 10 from 5/3/96 to 11/3/97." gopher://gopher.anc.org.za Human Rights Committee Documents/1997/Human Rights Update for Week No. 10 (1 Jan. 1998).

SCIENTIFIC STYLE

List the author's name (if known), last name first and then initials; the date of publication or last revision (if known), in parentheses; the title of the paper or file, capitalizing only the first word and any proper nouns; and the title of the complete work (if applicable), in italics and capitalized as just described. Include any previous publication information if applicable, then cite the protocol (i.e., "gopher"), the address, the gopher search path or directories followed to access the information; and, in parentheses immediately after the gopher path, the date accessed.

> Author's Last Name, Initial(s). (Date of publication or last revision). Title of document or file. *Title of complete work or gopher site.* Protocol and address and path or directories (date of access).

For example, for files accessed using a Web browser, a citation using the unique URL for the actual file might be:

> Perry, T. The quick and dirty guide to Japanese. gopher://hoshi.cic.sfu.ca:70/00/dlam/misc/Japanes.lang (12 Jun. 1997).

Pointing to the address of the main page and indicating the links that were followed to access the document, the citation becomes:

> Perry, T. The quick and dirty guide to Japanese. gopher://hoshi.cic.sfu.ca:70/ David See-Chai Lam Centre for International Communication/Miscellaneous Resources/THE QUICK AND DIRTY GUIDE TO JAPANESE (12 Jun. 1997).

2.10.2 Citing Books and Documents

Books and documents published electronically constitute a unique edition of the work. For works that have been previously published, you may want to include previous publication information, if available. It is important, however, to include as much information as possible about the electronic edition, including any identifying file numbers and electronic publication dates, in addition to the electronic address.

2.10.2.1 Citing original works

HUMANITIES STYLE

Give the author's name and the title of the work (that of a complete work in italics; that of a smaller work enclosed in quotation marks), including any previous print publication information (if applicable); the title of the electronic file, enclosed in quotation marks, if different from the original title; the file number, version number, file name, or other identifying information; the electronic publication date or date of last revision or modification; the title of the database (if applicable), in italics; the protocol and address; any paths or directories needed to access the work; and the date accessed, enclosed in parentheses.

> Ferber, Edna. *One Basket.* "The Project Gutenberg Etext of *One Basket,* by Edna Ferber." Etext #489. April 1996. *Project Gutenberg.* gopher://gopher.etext.org:70/00/Gutenberg/etext96/1bskt10.txt (14 Aug. 1996).

SCIENTIFIC STYLE

Give the author's last name and initial(s); the date of the work if different from the date accessed; the title of the work; any print publication information; the title of the electronic file (if different from the original title); the file number, version number, file name, or other identifying information (if applicable), enclosed in parentheses; the name of the database (if applicable), in italics; the protocol and address; and the date accessed, in parentheses.

> Ferber, E. (1996). *One basket.* The Project Gutenberg etext of *One basket,* by Edna Ferber. (Etext #489). *Project Gutenberg.* gopher://
> gopher.etext.org:70/00/Gutenberg/etext96/1bskt10.txt (14 Aug.1996).

2.10.2.2 Citing previously published works

For works with previous publication information, include as much information on the original publication as possible, followed by the electronic publication information.

HUMANITIES STYLE

List the author's name, the title (that of a shorter work enclosed in quotation marks; that of a book or anthology in italics), followed by the usual print publication information. Next, give the title of the electronic version if different from the print version; any identifying file or version numbers or the file name; the date of electronic publication; the name of the electronic publication site (if applicable), in italics; the protocol and address; any paths or directories necessary to access the work; and the date accessed, enclosed in parentheses.

> Cicero. "Pro Archia." *Select Orations of Cicero.* Ed. J. B. Greenough.
> Boston: Ginn, 1896. Ver. 0.01. Aug. 1994. *Project Libellus.* gopher://
> gopher.etext.org:/0/00/Libellus/texts/cicero/archia (14 Aug. 1996).

SCIENTIFIC STYLE

List the author's last name and initial(s), the date of publication in parentheses, and the original publication information. Follow with the title of the electronic version, in italics, if different from the print version; any identifying file or version numbers; the date of electronic publication, in parentheses; the site title; the protocol and address, including directory path (if applicable); and the date accessed, in parentheses.

> Cicero. (1896). Pro archia. In J. B. Greenough (Ed.), *Select orations of Cicero.* Boston: Ginn. (Version 0.01). (1994). *Project Libellus.* gopher://gopher.etext.org Libellus/texts/cicero/archia (11 Aug. 1996).

2.11 Information Available Using File Transfer Protocols (FTP)

FTP, or File Transfer Protocol, is a means of storing and accessing files on the Internet. Many FTP sites allow anonymous logins (where users use the login name "anonymous" and their email address as a password), and there are many different client programs available to access these sites. Like gopher sites, FTP sites can be accessed using Web browsers as well. They are also usually set up using a directory structure similar to gopher sites and should be cited in the same way. To cite files accessed using a browser, list the unique URL for the document or file, if available. Do not try to translate directory paths into a URL; if necessary, list the protocol and address for the main site and the links or directories followed to access the file.

2.11.1 General Format

HUMANITIES FORMAT

Give the author's name (if known), last name first; the full title (of a shorter work in quotation marks; of a larger work, in italics); and the document date (if available). Next, give the protocol (i.e., "ftp") and the full FTP address, including the full path needed to access the file. Last, list the date of access, enclosed in parentheses.

> Author's Last Name, First Name. "Title of Work." *Title of Complete Work.* Date of document. Protocol and address, path or directories (date of access).

The following example cites a document with a unique URL:

Johnson-Eilola, Johndan. "Little Machines: Rearticulating Hypertext Users." 5 Dec. 1994. ftp://ftp.daedalus.com/pub/CCCC95/johnson-eilola (14 Aug. 1996).

Citing the document in terms of links from a main FTP site, the citation would become:

Johnson-Eilola, Johndan. "Little Machines: Rearticulating Hypertext Users." 5 Dec. 1994. ftp://ftp.daedalus.com/ pub/CCCC95/johnson-eilola (14 Aug. 1996).

Notice that a single blank space is used to separate the directory path from the URL.

SCIENTIFIC FORMAT

Give the author's last name and initials; the document date (if known), in parentheses; the title of the document or file; the title of the complete work (if applicable), in italics; any previous publication information; the protocol and address; the directory path; and, in parentheses, date of access.

Author's Last Name, Initial(s). (Date). Title of work. *Title of complete work.* Protocol and address, directory path (date accessed).

The following example cites a document accessed using a Web browser:

Johnson-Eilola, J. (1994). Little machines: Rearticulating hypertext users. ftp://ftp.daedalus.com/pub/CCCC95/johnson-eilola (14 Aug. 1996).

When referencing a document in terms of links from a main FTP site, the citation becomes:

Johnson-Eilola, J. (1994). Little machines: Rearticulating hypertext users. ftp://ftp.daedalus.com/ pub/CCCC95/johnson-eilola (14 Aug. 1996).

2.11.2 Previously Published Works

Many electronic texts have been previously published, either on other electronic sites or in print form. If previous publication information is known, it should be included in the citation. It is still important, however, to cite the online version if this is the edition you have used.

2.11.2.1 Journals and magazines

HUMANITIES STYLE

To cite a paper previously published in a scholarly journal or a magazine, list the reference as you normally would for print publication, followed by the online publication information, including the title of the FTP site (if applicable), in italics; the protocol and address; the directory path; and the access date, in parentheses. You may, of course, omit any information, such as page numbers, that is not available.

Roush, Wade. "Have Computer, Won't Travel." *Technology Review Magazine* Feb. 1993. *MIT Media Laboratory FTP Server.* ftp:// media.mit.edu/pub/MediaMOO/Papers/Roush-Have-Computer-Won%27t-Travel (11 Aug. 1996).

SCIENTIFIC STYLE

Give the original publication information (if available), and continue with the online publication information, including the protocol and address, along with any path or directory commands necessary to access the work, and the date accessed, in parentheses. Omit information, such as page numbers, that is unavailable, but include as much as you can.

Minsky, M. (1982, Fall). Why people think computers can't think. *AI Magazine, 3*(4). ftp://publications.ai.mit.edu/classic-hits/minsky/ComputersCantThink (23 Dec. 1997).

2.11.2.2 Books

HUMANITIES STYLE

For files previously published in books, give the usual print publication information, followed by the online publication information, including the title, if different; any version or file numbers; the date of electronic publication; the name of the site, in italics; the protocol and address; the directory path; and the access date, in parentheses.

Cicero. "Pro Archia." *Select Orations of Cicero.* Ed. J. B. Greenough. Boston: Ginn, 1896. Ver. 0.01. 1 Aug. 1994. *Project Libellus.* ftp://ftp.etext.org/pub/Libellus/texts/cicero/archia.tex.gz (11 Aug. 1996).

SCIENTIFIC STYLE

Give the print publication information, if available, followed by the online publication information, including the electronic text title if different from the original title; any version or file numbers; the electronic publication date; the title of the electronic site, in italics; the protocol and address; the directory path; and, in parentheses, the access date.

Cicero. (1896). Pro archia. In J. B. Greenough (Ed.), *Select orations of Cicero* (Version 0.01). (1994, August 1). *Project Libellus.* ftp://ftp.etext.org/pub/Libellus/texts/cicero/archia.tex.gz (11 Aug. 1996).

2.11.2.3 Papers presented at conferences

HUMANITIES STYLE

List the author's name, last name first, and the title of the paper, enclosed in quotation marks. Continue with the words "Paper presented at" and the name of the conference, the location, and the date (if known). Then list the protocol and address, the directory path, and, in parentheses, the date accessed.

> Bruckman, Amy. "Democracy in Cyberspace." Paper presented at
> DIAC 94, Cambridge, MA, 23–24 Apr. 1994.
> ftp://ftp.media.mit.edu/pub/asb/papers/democracy-diac94.txt (11
> Aug. 1996).

SCIENTIFIC STYLE

List the last name and initials of the author(s); the date of presentation, in parentheses; the title of the paper; the words "Paper presented at" followed by the name of the conference and the conference location; the protocol and address; the directory path; and, in parentheses, the date accessed.

> Curtis, P., & Nichols, D. A. (1993, May 15). MUDs grow up:
> Social virtual reality in the real world. Paper presented at Third
> International Conference on Cyberspace, Austin, TX.
> ftp://lambda.moo.mud.org/pub/MOO/papers/MUDsGrowUp.txt
> (23 Dec. 1997).

2.11.3 Online Books

HUMANITIES STYLE

List the author's name, last name first; the title of the book, in italics; any print publication information; any identifying file numbers; and the electronic publication date (if known and if different from the date of access). Follow with the name of the online publication site (if applicable), in italics; the protocol and address; the directory path; and, in parentheses, the date of access.

> Hawthorne, Nathaniel. *Twice Told Tales.* Etext #508. Apr. 1996.
> *UIArchive.*

ftp://uiarchive.cso.uiuc.edu/pub/etext/gutenberg/etext96/2tale10.
txt (11 Aug. 1996).

SCIENTIFIC STYLE

List the author's last name and initials (if known); the publication
date, in parentheses; the title of the book, in italics; any print publication information (if known); the title of the electronic version
(if different), in italics; any version or identifying file numbers; the
title of the electronic site (if applicable), in italics; the protocol
and address; and the date of access, in parentheses.

U.S. Central Intelligence Agency. (1995). *The world factbook.*
Washington, DC: CIA. *The project Gutenberg etext of the 1995 CIA
world fact book. UIArchive.*
ftp://uiarchive.cso.uiuc.edu/pub/etext/gutenberg/etext96/world95.
txt (17 Aug. 1996)

2.12 Information Available Using Telnet Protocols

Telnet protocols allow the user to access information from a remote computer. Usually, telnet sites require users to have a login
name and a password, but many also allow guest access. URLs are
quickly becoming the standard way to cite Internet addresses;
however, although many browsers have the capability to access
telnet sites, not all users have access to Web browsers, and not all
Web browsers are configured to use telnet protocols. To access
these sites using a command-line interface rather than a browser
(for instance, using a Unix shell account), the user types the protocol (i.e., "telnet"), followed by a space, the address of the site,
followed by another space, and the port number. For example,
"telnet daedalus.com 7777."

The following examples give the addresses in the formats used
to access telnet sites with a browser (telnet://). However, because

there will be some differences in the address depending on how you access a site, it is important that you give the exact address and path you followed when accessing the information, rather than trying to convert the address from one form to another.

2.12.1 General Format

HUMANITIES STYLE

List the author's name or alias, last name first (if known); the title of the work (if applicable), in quotation marks; the title of the full work or telnet site (if applicable), in italics; the date of publication or creation (if known); and finally the protocol (i.e., "telnet") and complete telnet address, any directions necessary to access the publication, and the date of the visit, enclosed in parentheses. Separate commands from the address with a single blank space.

> Author's Last Name, First Name. "Title of Work." *Title of Complete Work*. Protocol and address and path (date of access).

For example, if you are using a Web browser:

> traci (#377). "DaedalusMOO Purpose Statement." *WriteWell*. telnet://moo.daedalus.com:7777 help purpose (30 Apr. 1996).

Using a command-line interface, this example would be:

> traci (#377). "DaedalusMOO Purpose Statement." *WriteWell*. telnet moo.daedalus.com 7777 help purpose (30 Apr. 1996).

SCIENTIFIC STYLE

List the author's last name and initial(s) or alias (if known); the date of publication (if known and if different from the date accessed), in parentheses; the title of the work; the title of the site or complete work (if applicable), in italics; and the protocol and complete telnet address, including the port number (if applicable), any necessary directions to access the publication, and the date of the visit, enclosed in parentheses.

> Author's Last Name, Initial(s). (Document Date). Title of work. *Title of site or complete work.* Protocol and address and command sequence (date of access).

For example, if you are using a web browser:

> traci (#377). DaedalusMOO purpose statement. *WriteWell.* telnet://moo.daedalus.com:7777 help purpose (30 Apr. 1996).

This example using raw telnet would become:

> traci (#377). DaedalusMOO purpose statement. *WriteWell.* telnet moo.daedalus.com 7777 help purpose (30 Apr. 1996).

2.12.2 No Author or Owner Listed

HUMANITIES STYLE

List the title of the document, enclosed in quotation marks; the name of the complete work or telnet site (if applicable), in italics; the date of publication or creation (if applicable); and finally the protocol, address, and port number, along with any commands necessary to access the information and, enclosed in parentheses, the date of access.

> "Welcome to *LambdaMOO." LambdaMOO.* telnet://lambda.parc. xerox.com:7777 (9 Aug. 1996).

SCIENTIFIC STYLE

List the title of the document; in parentheses, the publication or creation date if different from the access date; the name of the tel-net site (if applicable), in italics; and the protocol, address, and port number, along with any commands necessary to access the information and, in parentheses, the date of access.

Creating a Web page in a MOO. (1996). *DaMOO.*
telnet://damoo.csun.edu:7777 read #1101 (16 Aug. 1996).

2.12.3 Command Sequences

Command sequences are the commands the user must enter in order to access the information being cited; therefore, like directories or paths, they are important elements of the citation. Include necessary commands after the telnet address, separated by commas.

HUMANITIES STYLE

"Elsie the MOOteach RoboCow." *Diversity University.*
telnet://moo.du.org:8888 @go MOOteach, activate Elsie, say index (9 Aug. 1996).

SCIENTIFIC STYLE

Elsie the MOOteach robocow. *Diversity University.*
telnet://moo.du.org:8888 @go MOOteach, activate Elsie, say index (9 Aug. 1996).

2.12.4 Rooms, Objects, and Characters

Please note that object numbers are an important part of an object's name: in many programs it is possible to change names with alarming frequency, but the object's number will always remain the same.

HUMANITIES STYLE

List the owner of the object as the author (you may include the owner's object number, if applicable); the name and object number of the object (if known), in quotation marks; the title of the site (if applicable), in italics; and the protocol, address, and command sequence, followed by the date of access, enclosed in parentheses.

Hacker (#37). "The Reference Department (#127)." Internet Public Library MOO. telnet://ipl.sils.umich.edu:8888 @go #127 (11 Aug. 1996).

List the owner of the object as the author (include the owner's object number in parentheses, if applicable); the date created (if known), in parentheses; the name and object number of the object; the title of the site (if applicable), in italics; and the protocol, address, and command sequence, followed by the date accessed in parentheses.

Hacker (#37). The reference department (#127). *Internet Public Library MOO.* telnet://ipl.sils.umich.edu:8888 @go #127 (11 Aug. 1996).

2.12.5 Programming Code

If you are citing the entire program, give the name of the author and object number (if applicable); the name of the verb or program, in quotation marks; the name of the site (if applicable), in italics; the date of creation or last modification (if known); the protocol and address; the command sequence; and the date accessed, in parentheses. If you are citing specific lines of the program, include the line number or numbers in the in-text citation.

Tulkas (#141). "Say." *DaMOO.* 13 May 1996. telnet://damoo.csun.edu:7777 @list #3:say (23 Dec. 1997).

If you are citing the entire program, give the name and object number of the author (if known); the date of creation or last modification (if known), in parentheses; the name of the verb or program; the name of the site (if applicable), in italics; the protocol and address; the command sequence; and the date accessed, in parentheses. If you are citing specific lines of the program, include the line number or numbers in the in-text citation.

Tulkas (#141). (1996, May 13). Say. *DaMOO.*
telnet://damoo.csun.edu:7777 @list #3:say (23 Dec. 1997).

2.12.6 Note Objects

HUMANITIES STYLE

To cite a note object accessed via telnet protocols, list the owner or author's name or alias; the title and object number of the note object, enclosed in quotation marks; the title of the site, in italics; the date of creation or last modification (if known); the protocol and address; the command sequence; and, in parentheses, the date of access.

Kairos (#2084). "Fanning the Flames (#1322)." *DaMOO.*
telnet://damoo.csun.edu:7777 read #1322 (11 Aug. 1996).

SCIENTIFIC STYLE

List the owner or author's name or alias; the date created or last modified (if known), in parentheses; the title and object number of the note object; the title of the site, in italics; and the protocol and address, command sequence, and, in parentheses, date of access.

Kairos (#2084). Fanning the flames (#1322). *DaMOO.*
telnet://damoo.lrc.csun.edu:7777 read #1300 (11 Aug. 1996).

2.12.7 Mail Lists

Cite MOO and MUD mail messages as you would other electronic mail.

HUMANITIES STYLE

List the name or alias of the author; the subject line of the posting; the date of the message, in parentheses, if different from the date accessed; and the name and number of the list (if applicable). Then cite the name of the telnet site, in italics; the protocol and address; any commands necessary to access the message; and the date accessed, in parentheses.

Dava (#472). "A Deadline." 3 Nov. 1995. *General (#554). *Internet Public Library MOO.* telnet://ipl.sils.umich.edu:8888 @peek 25 on #554 (9 Aug. 1996).

SCIENTIFIC STYLE

List the name or alias of the author; the message date, in parentheses, if different from the date accessed; the subject line of the posting; the name and number of the list (if applicable); the title of the site (if applicable); and the protocol and address for the site, followed by any commands necessary to access the message, and the date accessed, in parentheses.

Dava (#472). (1995, November 3). A deadline. *General (#554). *Internet Public Library MOO.* telnet://ipl.sils.umich.edu:8888 @peek 25 on #554 (9 Aug. 1996).

2.12.8 Personal Email Messages

Cite personal mail messages as for electronic mail.

HUMANITIES STYLE

List the author's name or alias; the subject line from the message; the message date, if different from the date accessed; the type of communication (i.e., "Personal email"); the title of the site (if applicable), in italics; and the protocol and address, followed by the date accessed, in parentheses.

Max (#11113). "Planet Maps." 31 Jul. 1996. Personal email. *DaMOO.* telnet://lrc.csun.edu:7777 (24 Aug. 1996).

SCIENTIFIC STYLE

Cite the author's name or alias; the date of the message, in parentheses, if different from the date accessed; and the subject line from the posting. Then list the type of communication (i.e., "Personal email"), in square brackets; the site title (if applicable), in italics; and the protocol and address, followed by the date accessed, in parentheses.

> yduJ (#552). (1996, May 28). Comparisons [Personal email].
> *MediaMOO.* telnet://purple-crayon.media.mit.edu:8888 (13 Sep. 1996).

2.13 Synchronous Communication Sites

Synchronous communication sites are sites that allow multiple users to be connected at the same time and to communicate with each other, usually by typing text messages in real time. Whether you are keeping an electronic log or transcript of the session or simply taking notes, you should obtain permission from participants before using these conversations in your work. Synchronous communications may include personal interviews, online conferences, and other real-time discussions.

2.13.1 General Format

HUMANITIES STYLE

Include the name or alias of the author or speaker (if known); the type of communication (i.e., "Personal interview") or, for synchronous conferences, the session title (if applicable), enclosed in quotation marks; the site title (if applicable), in italics; the protocol and address, including any paths or directories, the command sequence (if applicable), and, in parentheses, the date of the conversation.

Author's Last Name, First Name (or alias). Type of communication or "Session Title." *Site Title.* Protocol and address and path or directories (date of access).

For example:

Kiwi. "Playing the Jester Is Hard Work." *DaMOO.* telnet://damoo.csun.edu:7777 (4 Dec. 1996).

SCIENTIFIC STYLE

Include the name or alias of the author or speaker (if known); the type of communication (e.g., Personal interview) or, for conferences, the session title; the site title (if applicable), in italics; the protocol and address, the command sequence (if applicable), and, in parentheses, the date of the conversation.

Author's Last Name, Initial(s) (or alias). Type of communication or session title. *Site title.* Protocol and address and command sequence (date of conversation).

For example:

Kiwi. Playing the jester is hard work. *DaMOO.* telnet://damoo.csun.edu:7777 (4 Dec. 1996).

2.13.2 Personal Interviews

HUMANITIES STYLE

Give the name of the speaker(s) (if applicable); the type of communication (Personal interview); the site title (if applicable), in italics; and the protocol, address or channel (if applicable), and, in parentheses, the date of communication.

Maxwell. Personal interview. *DaMOO.* telnet://damoo.csun.edu:7777 (4 Aug. 1996).

Oui. Personal interview. irc undernet.org@#help (13 Jan. 1996).

SCIENTIFIC STYLE

Give the name of the speaker(s) or alias; type of communication (Personal interview); the site title (if applicable), in italics; the protocol and address; the command sequence (if applicable); and, in parentheses, the date of the conversation. (See also 2.9.4.)

> Maxwell [guest]. Personal interview. *BioMOO.* telnet://
> bioinformatics.weizmann.ac.il:8888 (13 Jun. 1997).

> Oui. Personal interview. irc undernet.org@#help (13 Jan. 1996).

2.13.3 Online Conferences in Synchronous Communication

HUMANITIES STYLE

Give the name or alias of the speaker (if applicable); the session title, enclosed in quotation marks; and the title of the conference or site title (if applicable), in italics. Next, list the protocol (i.e., "telnet") and the complete telnet address, including the port number (if applicable), followed by any necessary commands to access the site. Separate the commands from the telnet address with a single blank space. Conclude with the date of the conference, in parentheses. Note: for sites that allow guest connections, it is not necessary to list the connection commands if these are displayed on the login screen.

> JaniceW. "What Are People Doing in Their Classes Next Semester?"
> *Netoric's Tuesday Cafe. MediaMOO.* telnet://purple-crayon.media.
> mit.edu:8888 @go Tuesday (6 Dec. 1994).

SCIENTIFIC STYLE

Give the name or alias of the speaker (if applicable); the session title; the title of the conference or site title, in italics (if applicable); the protocol and address, followed by any necessary commands to access the site; and, in parentheses, the date of the conference. For sites that allow guest connections, it is not necessary to list the connection commands if these are displayed on the login screen.

> JaniceW. What are people doing in their classes next semester? *Netoric's Tuesday cafe.Media MOO.* telnet://purple-crayon.media. mit.edu:8888 @go Tuesday (6 Dec. 1994).

2.13.4 Archived Conference Transcripts

HUMANITIES STYLE

List the author's name or alias, last name first (if known); the title of the file, enclosed in quotation marks; and the title of the conference, in italics. Then list the date of the conference and any file number or other identifying information. Continue with the title of the archive, in italics; the protocol used to access the archive (i.e., "ftp"); and the complete address, including the path or directories needed to access the file. Conclude with the date of access, enclosed in parentheses.

> JaniceW. "Why Use MUDs in the Writing Classroom?" *Netoric's Tuesday Cafe. MediaMOO.* 27 Feb. 1996. tc022796.log. *Daedalus Group Customer Support FTP Server.* ftp://ftp.daedalus.com/pub /ACW/NETORIC/Tuesday_Cafe_log.27Feb (14 Aug. 1996).

SCIENTIFIC STYLE

List the author's name or alias (if known); the date of the conference, in parentheses; the title of the file (if there is no author listed, follow the file title with the date of the conference); the title of the conference and/or site title, in italics, and any identifying file numbers or other information, enclosed in parentheses. Continue with the title of the archive site, if applicable, and then conclude with the protocol and address of the archive site and, in parentheses, the date of access.

JaniceW. (1996, February 27). Why use MUDs in the writing
classroom? *Netoric's Tuesday cafe. MediaMOO* (tc022796.log).
*Daedalus Group Customer Support FTP Server.*ftp://ftp.daedalus.
com/pub/ACW/NETORIC/Tuesday_ Cafe_log.27Feb (14 Aug.
1996).

2.13.5 BBS Chat Rooms

HUMANITIES STYLE

Give the name or alias of the speaker; the name of the chat room,
enclosed in quotation marks; and the name of the bulletin board
service, in italics. Then list the path followed to access the chat room
(if applicable) and the date of the conversation, in parentheses.

Tch Tanya. "Main Tutoring Room." *America Online.* Reference
Help/Academic Assistance Center (14 May 1996).

SCIENTIFIC STYLE

Give the name or alias of the speaker, the name of the chat room,
and, in italics, the name of the bulletin board service. Then list the
path followed to access the chat room, and, in parentheses, the
date of conversation.

Tch Tanya. Main tutoring room. *America Online.* Reference Help/
Academic Assistance Center (14 May 1996).

2.14 Online Reference Sources

Many reference works are now online, including interactive ency-
clopedias, dictionaries, thesauri, and style manuals. Some of these
are available only through subscriber services, such as BBSs, while
others are free for anyone to access. It is essential to distinguish
among Internet sources, BBS sources, and other subscriber services.

2.14.1 General Format

HUMANITIES STYLE

Give the author's name (if known); the title of the article, in quotation marks; the title of the complete work, in italics; any print publication information, including the date; information concerning the online edition (if applicable); the name of the online service, in italics, or the protocol and address and the path or directories followed; and, in parentheses, the date of access.

> Author's Last Name, First Name. "Title of Article." *Title of Complete Work*. Previous publication information and date. Online edition. *Online Service* or protocol and address and any paths or directories (date accessed).

For example:

> "Fine Arts." *Dictionary of Cultural Literacy.* 2nd ed. Ed. E. D. Hirsch, Jr., Joseph F. Kett, and James Trefil. Boston: Houghton Mifflin, 1993. INSO Corp. *America Online.* Reference Desk/Dictionaries/ Dictionary of Cultural Literacy (20 May 1996).

SCIENTIFIC STYLE

Give the author's last name and initials; the publication date (if known and if different from the date accessed); and the title of the article. Then cite the word "In," followed by the name(s) of the author(s) or editor(s) (if applicable) and, in italics, the title of the complete work; any previous print publication information (if applicable); identification of the online edition (if applicable); the name of the online service, in italics, or the protocol and address and the path followed to access the material; and, in parentheses, the date accessed.

> Author's Last Name, Initial(s). (Date). Title of article. In *Title of complete work.* Previous publication information. Identification of

online edition if applicable. *Online service* or protocol and address and path or directories (date accessed).

For example:

Fine arts. (1993). In E. D. Hirsch, Jr., J. F. Kett, & J. Trefil (Eds.), *Dictionary of cultural literacy.* Boston: Houghton Mifflin. INSO Corp. *America Online.* Reference Desk/Dictionaries/Dictionary of Cultural Literacy (20 May 1996).

2.14.2 No Author Listed

HUMANITIES STYLE

List the title of the article, in quotation marks; the title of the encyclopedia or reference work, in italics; any print publication information; the name of the online service, in italics, or the protocol and address for Internet sources and the path or directories followed to access the source; and the date accessed, in parentheses.

"Artificial Intelligence." *Compton's Living Encyclopedia.* Compton's, 1995. *America Online.* Reference Desk/Encyclopedias/Compton's (14 May 1996).

SCIENTIFIC STYLE

List the title of the article; the date of publication (if known and if different from the date accessed), in parentheses; the word "In" followed by the title of the encyclopedia, in italics; any previous print publication information; any online edition identification; the title of the online service, in italics, or the protocol and address and the paths or directories followed to access the work; and, in parentheses, the date accessed.

Artificial intelligence. (1995). In *Compton's living encyclopedia.* Compton's. *America Online.* Reference Desk/Encyclopedias/ Compton's (14 May 1996).

2.14.3 Print Publication Information Included

HUMANITIES STYLE

List the author's name (if known); the title of the article, in quotation marks; and the title of the encyclopedia or reference source, in italics. Continue with any print publication information, including the city, publisher, and date (if applicable). Include the name of the electronic publisher after the print publication information, and then list the name of the online service or the Internet protocol and address followed by the path or directories to access the source and, in parentheses, the date accessed.

> "Australia." *The Concise Columbia Encyclopedia*. 3rd ed. New York: Columbia UP, 1994. INSO Corp. *America Online*. Reference Desk/Encyclopedias/Columbia Concise (20 May 1996).

SCIENTIFIC STYLE

List the author's last name and initials (if known); the date of publication; the title of the article; the word "In" followed by the title of the encyclopedia or reference source, in italics; and any print publication information, including the place of publication and the publisher's name (if applicable). Then cite the electronic publication information, including the title of the electronic work, if different; the name of the electronic publisher; the name of the online service or the protocol and address and any paths or directories; and, in parentheses, the date accessed. For works with no listed author, begin with the title of the article followed by the publication date, in parentheses.

> Australia. (1994). In *The concise Columbia encyclopedia* (3rd ed.). NY: Columbia UP. INSO Corp. *America Online*. Reference Desk/Encyclopedias/Columbia Concise (20 May 1996).

2.15 Electronic Publications and Online Databases

Some books and reference sources are published on CD-ROM or diskettes or may be available only from certain computer terminals. Computerized library catalogs may include sources from online information services that are only available by subscription, or your library may have subscriptions to CD-ROM information services. Include in citations as much information as possible on the software or information service used to access information.

2.15.1 General Format

HUMANITIES STYLE

List the author's name, last name first (if known); the title of the article, in quotation marks; and the title of the software publication, in italics. Next, list any version or edition numbers or other identifying information, the series name (if applicable), and the date of publication. Finally, cite the name of the database (if applicable) and the name of the online service—both in italics—or the Internet protocol and address, any other publication information, the directory path followed (if applicable), and, in parentheses, the date accessed.

> Author's Last Name, First Name. "Title of Article." *Title of Software Publication.* Publication information, including version or edition number, if applicable, and date of publication. *Name of database,* if applicable. *Name of online service* or Internet protocol and address. File or version number or other identifying information and directory path (date accessed).

For example:

Warren, Christopher. "Working to Ensure a Secure and

Comprehensive Peace in the Middle East." U.S. Dept. of State
Dispatch 7:14, 1 Apr. 1996. *FastDoc. OCLC.* File #9606273898
(12 Aug. 1996).

SCIENTIFIC STYLE

List the author's last name and initials; the date of publication, in
parentheses; the title of the article or file and, enclosed in parentheses, any identifying file or version numbers or other identifying
information (if applicable); the title of the electronic database, in
italics; the name of the online service, in italics, and access information or the protocol and address and any directory paths; and,
in parentheses, the date accessed.

> Author's Last Name, Initial(s). (Date). Title of article (Version or file
> number). *Title of database. Name of online service* and path, or
> protocol and address (file number). (Date accessed).

For example:

> Warren, C. (1996). Working to ensure a secure and comprehensive
> peace in the Middle East (U.S. Dept. of State Dispatch 7:14). *Fast
> Doc. OCLC* (File #9606273898). (12 Aug. 1996).

2.15.2 CD-ROM, Diskette, and Magnetic Tape

HUMANITIES STYLE

List the author's name, last name first; the title of the article, in
quotation marks; the title of the publication, in italics; any version
or edition numbers; the series name (if applicable); and the publication information (if available). Note that, for this type of publication, the date accessed is not included.

> Zieger, Herman E. "Aldehyde." *The Software Toolworks Multimedia
> Encyclopedia.* Vers. 1.5. Software Toolworks. Boston: Grolier, 1992.

SCIENTIFIC STYLE

List the author's last name and initials; the date of publication, in parentheses; the title of the article; the title of the publication; the version or file number, in parentheses; the series name; and the publication information, including city and publisher.

Zieger, H. (1992). Aldehyde. *The Software Toolworks multimedia encyclopedia* (Version 1.5). Software Toolworks. Boston: Grolier.

2.15.3 Computer Information Services and Online Databases

HUMANITIES STYLE

List the author's name; the title of the work, in quotation marks or italics as appropriate; any publication information (if applicable); the title of the information service or database, in italics; the publisher or retrieval service or the Internet protocol and address; and, in parentheses, the date of access.

Abdul-Ghani, Mohamed. "Comparison of the Effect of Instructional versus Industry-Specific Computer Simulation on Students Learning in a Front Office Management Course." *DAI* 56 (1996): 4363A. U of Tennessee, 1995. *Dissertation Abstracts Online. OCLC* (22 May 1996).

SCIENTIFIC STYLE

List the author's last name and initials; the date of publication, in parentheses; the title of the work; any print publication information, in parentheses; the title of the information service or database (if applicable), in italics; the name of the electronic publisher or retrieval service or the Internet protocol and address; and, in parentheses, the date of access.

Abdul-Ghani, M. (1996). Comparison of the effect of instructional versus industry-specific computer simulation on students learning in a front office management course (Doctoral dissertation, U of Tennessee, 1995. *Dissertation Abstracts International,* 56, 4363A). *Dissertation Abstracts Online. OCLC* (22 May 1996).

2.16 Software Programs and Video Games

When citing software programs and video games, it is important to give as much information as possible. Include the author of the software program or video game, the title of the game or software (in italics), the version or file number or other identifying information, the publisher of the software program, and the date of publication if known. The date accessed is not necessary when citing software and video game programs.

2.16.1 General Format

HUMANITIES STYLE

Cite the name of the author or corporate author (if available); the title of the software program, in italics; the version number (if applicable and if not included in the software title); and the publication information, including the date of publication (if known).

Author or Corporate Author. *Title of Software or Video Game.* Vers. City: Publisher, year of publication.

For example:

ID Software. *The Ultimate Doom.* New York: GT Interactive Software, 1995.

SCIENTIFIC STYLE

Cite the last name and initials of the author (if available); the date of publication or release, in parentheses; the title of the software program or video game, in italics; the version number (if applicable and if not included in the software title), in parentheses; and the publication information.

> Author's Last Name, Initial(s) (or corporate author). (Date). *Title of program* (Version). City: Publisher.

For example:

> ID Software. (1995). *The ultimate doom.* NY: GT Interactive Software.

2.16.2 Corporate Author as Publisher

When no individual author is listed and the corporate author and the publisher are the same, you may begin with the title of the software.

HUMANITIES STYLE

Follow the title of the software with the publication information.

> *WordPerfect Vers. 6.1 for Windows.* Ottawa, ON: Corel, 1996.

SCIENTIFIC STYLE

Follow the software title with the date of publication, in parentheses, and then the publication information.

> *WordPerfect Vers. 6.1 for Windows.* (1996). Ottawa, ON: Corel.

2.16.3 Citing Specific Information in a Software Program

HUMANITIES STYLE

List the title of the screen or document referenced, enclosed in quotation marks; the title of the software, in italics; the version or other identifying information (if applicable); the publication information; and any commands or path followed to access the information.

"Agent Provisions." *It's Legal for Windows*. Vers. 5.1. Parson's
Technology, 1994. Legal Guide/Powers of Attorney/Agent
Provisions.

SCIENTIFIC STYLE

List the title of the screen or document referenced; the date of
publication, in parentheses; the title of the software program; the
version number or other identifying information (if applicable),
in parentheses; the publication information; and any necessary
commands or directories followed to access the information.

Agent provisions. (1994). *It's Legal for Windows* (Version 5.1).
Parson's Technology. Legal Guide/Powers of Attorney/Agent
Provisions.

PART 2

Production

3

The Logic of Document Style

Style, in the broadest sense of the term, refers to a wide range of issues and standards for producing documents. It relates to decisions regarding syntax, word choice, sentence and paragraph structure, and figures of speech, as well as punctuation, spelling, capitalization, citation, and document format. Issues of syntax, word choice, figurative language, and sentence structure are particularly subjective. Consider the two very different styles illustrated in the following example: "I have wanted to become a doctor since high school" and "Becoming an M.D. has always been, for me, the pot of gold at the end of the rainbow." Neither of these ways of expressing the same thought is necessarily better than the other, and the appropriateness of one versus the other depends largely on context. The more technical and less poetic style would be more appropriate for an application to medical school, whereas the more figurative style might make for a better short story.

The next two chapters do not discuss style in terms of syntax, word choice, and figures of speech; guides to grammar are typically the best source of advice on these matters. These chapters also do not address, for the most part, spelling, punctuation, and capitalization, because other, more comprehensive guides, such as *The Chicago Manual of Style,* have already formulated effective standards for issues of that sort. Instead, we focus on establishing standards for formal academic style that accommodate changing electronic technologies.

Like the logic of citation style, the logic of document style is based primarily on the desire to facilitate the process of knowledge building. Standardized document style supports this process in a number of ways: by providing familiar structures and hierarchies for organizing information so that texts are more readable, by streamlining the complex task of producing documents in a way that saves time and clerical costs, and by coordinating formats among authors and disciplines so that texts may be more easily compared with one another. These advantages help authors and readers to orient texts so that they are more readable and easier and cheaper to produce, purchase, and circulate.

Like citation style, effective document style adheres to the principles of access, intellectual property, economy, standardization, and transparency (see the discussion in chapter 1), although these principles are slightly modified when considering document style. For citation, the principle of access required that a citation style make locating cited sources as effortless as possible. In terms of document style, the principle of access requires that the author format a document in such a way that it is easily cited, archived, and indexed for retrieval purposes. Thus citation style and document style are intimately connected; for example, one of the primary reasons to indicate clearly the title of a document, the name(s) of its author(s), and the location of the file or document within the document itself is so that it can be cited effectively. One significant problem with much of the material stored online today is that there are no standards for indicating titles, names of authors, and section or page numbers, thereby making it difficult not only to cite information but also to access material in the first place. Another factor contributing to the problem of access online is that institutionalized archives with a high degree of reliability have yet to be established on the Internet. Authors are often unable to ensure that their documents will remain in the same place for a long period of time—an obvious transgression of the principle of access.

Document style is also based on the principle of economy: documents should be formatted to minimize the amount of time required to read a document as well as the amount of labor required to produce the text in a readable form or to store the file electronically. For example, large electronic files are time-consuming to load, which violates the principle of economy.

Document style, like citation style, is, in fact, an abbreviated code that conveys information by using spacing and changes in fonts to indicate titles and subheadings; italics, boldface, underlining, and color to indicate emphasis or titles (or links in hypertext documents); and numbers located in margins to indicate page numbers or section numbers. In hypertext documents, the code may also employ image maps, blinking fonts, animated graphics, sound files, or embedded applications.

Examine, for instance, figure 3.1. At a quick glance we can tell that the name of this document's author is Brown, that we are looking at the second page of the text, that the image of women is the subtopic being discussed on this page, and that the work being cited is by a scholar named Prescott. We can also expect that the information required to locate the cited text will be provided in the bibliography of the document. All this important and necessary information is conveyed through formatting; that is, it is communicated by means of the shape and location of text in a document.

Like citation style, then, document style must also follow the principle of standardization, which requires that users all follow the same code so that they can understand each other. If authors and readers are to use document style to support effective knowledge building, they must employ and understand the standards on which the codified style is based.

Brown 2

in presenting women as archetypes.

Image of Women

A similar view sees Hemingway as making "use of feminist rhetoric of rage, economy of stereotype, and metonymic displacement to illuminate perceived gender and ethnic differences within a society that professes to foster equality yet frowns on difference" (Prescott 177). However, in placing women in this almost Christ-like position--the saviors of mankind as it were--is Hemingway presenting women at all? Or is he presenting only male fantasies--the kind of stereotypical, mythic female figure that women have been condemned by our society to try to live up to?

Figure 3.1 Sample Manuscript Page in MLA Format

Clearly, electronic and online documents present new possibilities for standards in addition to or perhaps instead of those supporting the principles of accessibility, intellectual property, economy, standardization, and transparency of style. Consider the use of hypertextual links as a formatting feature that can work alongside italics, boldface, subheadings, page numbers, and the like. If both a bibliography and a cited work are located on the World Wide Web, for example, then why not make the reference a hypertextual link to the cited work itself instead of merely listing the title in the bibliography? Doing so clearly supports the principles of access (the cited work is almost instantly available) and economy (the reader saves time traveling to and searching through a print library), as well as those of standardization and transparency (after five minutes online, even novices are likely to pick up on the code that indicates a hypertextual link to another online resource: these links are often a different color from body text and are usually underlined).

For these reasons, we must begin to consider how documents should be formatted to be stored electronically, typically on a magnetic disk or a hard drive, as well as how they should appear on a screen. We must address a set of new issues that probably never occurred to most writers of academic documents; for example, we now need to consider how to format our writing and store it so that it can be easily accessed and read by a wide variety of people using a wide variety of technologies. This extends the principle of access to mean that once an author composes a text and stores it electronically, that text should be readable, more or less, by any word processor or WWW browser on any conventional computer without the difficult, irritating, and often unsuccessful task of "translating" the text or file. According to the principle of access, not only should new standards for document style allow files to be read by most computers, but these standards should permit files on the Internet or the Web to appear onscreen more or less as the author intended when the file was created in the first place.

Thus document style has taken on a new dimension: making files compatible with a wide variety of technologies or platforms. But standards for achieving cross-platform compatibility must also accommodate the needs and logic of conventional, print-oriented document production styles during this period of transition between a print-oriented culture and a more fully electronic one. In the first two chapters we explained online citation style in terms of the generic components that make up most bibliographic citations: author, title, and publication information. Likewise, document style can also be explained in terms of generic components. Academic documents are typically easy to format because they are fairly austere. The styles they employ are intended to emphasize content and substance over flash. The components that constitute the core of academic document style are basic, hierarchical, and utilitarian.

As we noted in the preface of this book, the standardization of style may seem, on the one hand, like a top-down phenomenon in which powerful authorities determine rules that everyone else must follow. But, on the other hand, if rules or standards are to be effective and take hold, they must reflect the values and identity of a community of writers; thus standards are also determined from the ground up. The world of academic and scholarly publishing may very well be headed toward some consensus regarding online style. Large national and international organizations such as ANSI and ISO have been trying for some time now to generate logical, user-friendly guides to formatting electronic texts, and they have had some success in this pursuit, apparently moving in the direction of promoting SGML, which is an acronym for Standard Generalized Markup Language.

The recent widespread popularity of the World Wide Web might, however, counter attempts to establish SGML as the standard. HTML (Hypertext Markup Language), the current standard for the Web, was originally considered a subset of SGML. Because of the widespread popularity of the Web, however, HTML continues to expand in directions far beyond the official limits of SGML. Fortunately, in terms of producing academic documents, SGML and HTML are so similar that an author need only understand the basics of either of these standards in order to produce documents that follow the principle of access. Those who argue the superiority of SGML point out that the body responsible for establishing it is composed of highly skilled and well-researched authorities whose specific area of expertise is the creation and maintenance of such standards. Those who argue the superiority of HTML point out that market-driven forces have made HTML so popular and widely recognized that trying to bend people away from it and toward SGML is a waste of effort.

On the other side of the fence from those arguing about the relative merits of SGML, HTML, and the like are those who observe that the vast majority of writing being done on computers, especially in academic environments, is formatted on standard word processors such as *WordPerfect* and *Word*. There seems to be increasing consensus on the formats used by these word processors, and the latest versions of such software contain integrated translators that make it fairly easy to move back and forth from one brand of word processor to another, from one type of computer to another, and among formats such as text, SGML, and HTML. Why go to the trouble of leaping to formats such as SGML and HTML, which seem exotic, when the average writer can do all of his or her work on a conventional word processor?

Each of the arguments regarding word processors, SGML, and HTML is compelling, and the question as to which should be accepted as standard certainly remains to be resolved. In the meantime, however, academic and scholarly writers, editors, and publishers need advice on which option to pursue if they have a choice. We would argue that, all things considered, HTML is, at present, the best option because it holds the most potential for making the possibility of cross-platform translatability a reality in academic circles and because the downside to learning HTML is relatively small. If HTML fails to take hold and another language becomes the standard, the investment in learning HTML should not be a monumental loss for its users because future languages are likely to encompass, not contradict, its principles.

While the option of sticking with a standard word processor may sound appealing to many authors, editors and publishers are more apt to balk at this approach. No matter how effective or "clean" a program for translating between word processors and desktop publishing software may seem, there are always glitches. This means editors and publishers must develop elaborate and resource-consuming procedures for making sure that translations do not introduce errors, and this can be a nightmare. The problem of translating between word processing and desktop publishing software also creates problems for authors. Because most academic texts are now originally stored electronically by the authors and because rekeying an author's writing is an expensive and time-consuming process, many editors and publishers have procedures that they have developed in-house for submitting manuscripts electronically. Before the publication of this guide, no standardization of electronic academic texts existed, and authors often have had to take on the tedious and frustrating chore of first comprehending in-house guidelines and then trying to conform to them, a task that must be performed repeatedly because each publisher has different guidelines. *The Columbia Guide* can help solve this problem.

The guidelines that follow attempt to move authors, editors, and publishers alike toward consensus on the production of electronic manuscript submission. Chapter 4 discusses the proper preparation of texts in hard copy (paper) and electronic form; chapter 5 presents standards for document production for materials published on computer networks, especially the World Wide Web. Authors, teachers, and editors should decide which standard (word processing or network) best suits their needs and review the information in the appropriate chapter(s). Standards based on word processing applications are likely to be, at first, the most accommodating to teachers, students, and the typical scholarly author, although these standards are more limited in terms of transferring documents between applications and the Internet.

At present, individual editors, publishers, institutions, and associations all have their own specific guidelines for producing and formatting documents, and these guidelines must be carefully followed by authors wanting to submit a successful manuscript. These various guidelines are generally reasonable, well thought out, and useful; they help writers produce attractive documents relatively easily, and they encourage all writers to present clean and neat texts with ample margins, clearly labeled titles, logically organized subheadings, and prudently arranged bibliographies. However, in a world where liberality of access and cross-pollination of formats is becoming the norm, it would seem timely for journals and presses to consider adopting a single set of standards—such as those described in either chapter 4 and/or 5—as their in-house guidelines for submission of manuscripts on disk and in hard copy form so that both authors and publishers can begin to take advantage of more uniform processes for submission and publication.

4

Formats Intended for Print Publication

In this chapter we define standards for using word-processing software to produce hard-copy (i.e., paper) documents for submission either in print form only or in conjunction with electronic copy on disk or another electronic medium. These standards are designed to help two primary groups of people: (1) students and teachers who exchange written assignments and (2) authors, editors, and publishers who exchange documents and files intended for print publication. (Standards for producing documents to be published electronically are presented in chapter 5.)

Before getting into the specifics of these standards, we need to emphasize a cardinal rule regarding working with word processors to produce formal academic and scholarly papers on hard copy: *In all circumstances, keep it simple.*

For academic and scholarly documents that will be submitted to publishers either as hard copy or in electronic formats for print publication, this cardinal rule has two important corollaries:

Corollary 1: Do not use any of the word processor's formatting features unless you absolutely must. This means, do not change fonts, do not change margins, and do not justify text unless necessary to meet the demands of the person or organization receiving your work (for example, text on cover and title pages should be centered using the automatic-centering feature of your word processor; block quotations in print-only texts should be indented using the automatic-indentation feature, not by changing the margins; and some citation styles demand centered or boldface subheads). As long as the default settings on your word processor are reasonable, use them. By "reasonable" we mean that the default font should be Courier, Roman (or Times Roman, or Times New Roman), or Palatino (or the closest equivalent, if one of these is not available); the margins should generally be set to one inch on all sides (unless otherwise stipulated in the style guidelines you are following); the *entire* document should be double-spaced; and all text, except for inset quotations, page numbers, and inset lists, should be flush with the left-hand margin (i.e., left-justified). If the default settings on your word processor are inappropriate, change them.

Corollary 2: Do not invent new elements of document style. As we said earlier, academic and scholarly document style is essentially simple. Almost all academic authors really need only three special formatting features to produce a text: italics (or underlining if required to meet publisher's guidelines), automatic indent features, and automatic page numbering. In addition, authors who are required to use footnotes instead of endnotes should take advantage of automatic footnoting features, and authors required to provide bibliographies with hanging indents should take advantage of word processing features that help automate such indentation. For documents to be submitted in hard-copy form only (such as course essays), authors who have mastered automatic section numbering, list numbering, bulleting, and endnotes should also take advantage of these functions, although they should be aware that such automatic functions can create problems for the novice user and may sometimes be incompatible with some styles for citation. All authors should take advantage of spell checkers, although spell checkers will not replace careful proofreading.

For texts submitted in electronic format for print publication, a third corollary also applies:

Corollary 3: If you are an author who has been asked to submit your work in electronic form using a standard word processing application, be aware that every special formatting feature you employ in your text other than italics/underlining and page numbering is likely to have to be removed by your publisher and can easily introduce errors into your manuscript.

Do not worry that important elements of style such as block quotations, titles, and subheads will not be formatted effectively under these austere guidelines. Formatting codes, or tags, are used to designate these items. These code- or tag-based styles replace the standard styles for academic documents that rely on typographical systems for formatting texts and foster easier translation from one application (i.e., the author's word-processing program) to another (i.e., the publisher's electronic text-processing program) with the least possibility of error. For example, to distinguish a subhead in the interior of a text, conventional guides to style require that it be set off using a typographical formatting procedure, such as underlining or italics, that is also used for other purposes, such as indicating emphasis or foreign words. A code- or tag-based format, by contrast, is intended to generate a document in which the devices used to indicate different elements of style correspond specifically and logically to the elements themselves. For example, in this system, an author would not indicate a subhead with underlining or italics but instead would surround it with a pair of tags not only designating it as a subhead but specifying what type of subhead it is.

At first, acclimating to this new system for formatting may seem tedious and constrictive, but it will be liberating in the long run. Virtually every academic author knows the frustration of trying to format a particular document to meet the idiosyncratic demands of individual teachers, publishers, and editors. Consider, for example, the different approaches recommended by Chicago, APA, and MLA for formatting subheads in conventional typographical markup standards. Chicago and MLA prefer A-level subheads to be set flush left, in all capital letters, while APA requires that A-level subheads be centered, in upper- and lowercase letters. In a tag-based format, authors simply tag an A-level subhead with <H3> at the beginning of the head and </H3> at the end, and readers, publishers, and editors can arrange the subhead on the page or screen as they please. Thus authors who use a tag-based format need only familiarize themselves with one small list of tags for formatting the basic elements of an academic text; editors and publishers can then easily locate the tagged elements and, using global search-and-replace commands, recode them according to their preferences.

❋ ❋ ❋

Although keeping the cardinal rule of word processing and its corollaries in mind can solve a great many problems for authors, editors, and publishers, specific ramifications of these rules need to be spelled out. Table 4.1 presents a summary of the general rules to follow when using a word processor to prepare a document. More detailed explanations and rules for the individual components of document style follow.

THE PARTS OF THE TEXT

4.1 Front Matter

Front matter for chapter- and article-length texts can include a cover page, an abstract, and a preface or introduction. Book-length projects sometimes require additional front matter, for example, forewords, acknowledgments, and lists of artwork. Each element of front matter for book-length projects should be stored either separately as an independent file or collectively in a single file. Material for the cover of a book should always be stored as an independent file, never collected with the other front matter. The

TABLE 4.1

- For texts to be submitted in hard copy form only (such as academic coursework), use italics to designate book titles, emphasis, and foreign words. For texts to be submitted for print publication, use tags to designate formatting unless otherwise required by your publisher's style guidelines (many publishers require the use of underlining to designate text that will appear in italics in final published form).

- Use boldface *only* in the rare circumstance required by certain mathematical formulas.

- Use hard returns only to separate sections, subheads, block quotations, and paragraphs; never use them within paragraphs.

- Use a hard return and a single tab to separate and indent paragraphs.

- Use a double hard return and no tab to isolate each of the following elements when required: title, byline, notes, bibliographic entries.

- Never use tabs or the space bar to indent a block quotation. Do not use hard returns to separate the lines inside a block quotation. Use the word processor's automated indent function to inset text for print-only texts or use tags for texts to be submitted for print publication.

- If you must move text away from the left margin to create columns in a table, use tabs; do not use the space bar or change the margins.

- Do not center or fully justify text unless absolutely required to do so. If you must center some portions of your text (such as on the cover or title page) between the right and left margins, use the word processor's centering function (or tags for work to be submitted to publishers); never center manually using tabs or space bars.

other elements should be separated with hard page breaks (unless each is already located in a separate computer file).

The following elements are discussed in the order in which they would appear in the text.

4.1.1 Covers and Cover Pages

Cover

Covers are generally not the responsibility of the author, although authors sometimes provide dust jacket or back cover copy designed to promote the book. If this material is to be provided, it should be located in a file or on a disk separate from the rest of the manuscript. Since digital images tend to be relatively memory-consuming, digital files containing graphics for a cover provided by the author should be also placed on a separate disk from the rest of the manuscript.

Cover page

A cover page is a single page that contains at least the complete title of the work and the name(s) and affiliation(s) of the work's author(s), editor(s), and translator(s). Articles, essays, and chapters do not necessarily require cover pages; the title and the authors' names and affiliations can be placed on the first page of the manuscript. Center all text on the cover page in print-only texts; in texts to be submitted for print publication, however, place all text flush left and use tags to designate formatting.

Because academic papers are often submitted anonymously for the purposes of objective grading or review, a cover page may also need to include information for contacting or identifying the author, such as an address or a student identification number. In such cases, it is imperative that the title on the cover page correspond with the title and headers in the manuscript itself. Some style guides, such as APA, require that the running header be either included or indicated on the cover page.

If you must supply an abstract, you will need a cover page. But, in all other circumstances, do not use a cover page unless required to do so.

4.1.2 Title Page

In book-length texts, the title page contains as much of the following information as appropriate: full title of complete work; names of author(s), editor(s), or compiler(s); name(s) of translator(s); edition number; series name; volume number; name(s) of series editor(s); name and location of publisher.

4.1.3 Information Page

In book-length texts, the information page contains data relevant to the publishing and archiving of the manuscript. It typically includes such information as copyright and edition information—including dates of publication or copyright—name and address of publisher, Library of Congress Cataloging-in-Publication (CIP) data, and International Standard Book Number(s) (ISBN) or International Standard Serial Number(s) (ISSN).

4.1.4 Abstract or Summary

An abstract or summary should be an informative synopsis that captures the focus of a work, usually within the space of about two or three hundred words. Chapters in books do not need abstracts or summaries.

When formatting an abstract, locate it on a separate page or pages placed between the cover or title page and all following material (be sure to use hard page breaks to create these separations; do not use hard returns to move to the next page). Use the word "Abstract" as a chapter head to identify the abstract as such. See section 4.12.1 for the treatment of chapter and article titles in both print-only texts and those prepared in electronic form for print publication. Page numbers for abstracts often use Roman rather than Arabic numerals and are centered in the footer rather than being placed flush right in the header. If you must use Roman numerals and begin numbering the body text on page 1 (after the abstract), it may be easier to save and print out your abstract as a separate computer file.

4.1.5 Table of Contents

The table of contents, or contents page, is a list of the major divisions, sections, or chapters of a book-length manuscript or long report. It should clearly link the names of the major divisions with either the beginning page numbers or section numbers. Use a chapter head (see section 4.12.1) to designate the title of the page as appropriate (i.e., "Table of Contents" or "Contents"), and separate the page from other front matter or from the body of the text with a hard page break (for print-only text), or save it as a separate computer file.

Automatic functions for formatting contents pages (such as the automatic justification feature, with or without dot leaders, to place page numbers flush right) may be used for texts to be produced in print-only formats, as long as the author is comfortable with these software features, but most academic papers are so simple that manual formatting is relatively easy. Always double-check numbers on contents pages before submitting final copy.

4.1.6 List of Illustrations and Figures

This is a tabular list of all the titles of illustrations and figures that appear in the text, along with the corresponding page or section numbers in which or next to which these illustrations appear. This list is typically necessary only when a manuscript contains more than three or so illustrations. Code the title of the list (i.e., "List of Illustrations" or other appropriate title as indicated by the style you are following) as a chapter head (see section 4.12.1), and separate it from other parts of the front matter or from the body of the text with a hard page break or by saving it as a separate computer file.

4.1.7 List of Tables

This is a tabular list of the titles of all the tables that appear in the text, along with the corresponding beginning page or section numbers in which or next to which the tables appear. This list is typically necessary only when the manuscript contains more than three or so tables and should be formatted similarly to the list of illustrations.

4.1.8 Foreword

A foreword is a commentary in a book-length text that is usually written by someone other than the author; it discusses the project that follows. In general, code the word "Foreword" at the top of the page as a chapter head (see section 4.12.1). The foreword should be formatted the same as the rest of the body text, except that the author's name, title, and affiliation may be placed at the end of the foreword. Separate the foreword from other front matter or from the body of the text with a hard page break, or save it as a discrete computer file.

4.1.9 Acknowledgments

The acknowledgments are a chronicle of those individuals, institutions, and organizations that assisted in the creation of a manuscript. Acknowledgments are often included in the preface. Code the title of separate acknowledgments (e.g., "Acknowledgments") as a chapter head (see section 4.12.1), and separate the acknowledgments from the body of the text with a hard page break or by saving them as a discrete computer file.

4.1.10 Preface

A preface is a commentary written by the author(s) that discusses the project that follows. Prefaces typically contain information about the publication of the text, such as the history of the project, important contributors, or editions or translations of the text; such information may also be handled through an author's or editor's note.

When formatting a preface in a book-length text, use the word "Preface" as a chapter head to identify it as such (see section 4.12.1); when including a preface in an article-length text, format its title as an A-level subhead (see section 4.15). Use similar formatting as for the rest of the body text, and separate the preface from other front matter or from the body of the text with a hard page break or by saving it as a discrete computer file.

4.1.11 Introduction

An introduction is commentary written by the author(s) that discusses the project that follows. Unlike a preface, introductions typically orient the reader to the ensuing text's argument or content, usually including substantial information about the organization and theme of the text. However, no hard and fast rule can be said to distinguish the function of a preface from that of an introduction. It is highly unlikely that an article will require both a preface and an introduction, although this is not uncommon in book-length texts.

When formatting an introduction in a book-length text, locate it immediately before the body text. Use the word "Introduction" as a chapter head to identify the introduction as such (see section 4.12.1); when including an introduction in an article-length text, format its title as an A-level subhead (see section 4.15). Follow the same general formatting as for the preface.

4.2 Back Matter

The back matter for article-length texts includes the conclusion, appendixes, notes, and bibliography. Book-length manuscripts may also contain indexes, glossaries, lists of contributors, and other paraphernalia.

4.2.1 Conclusion

A conclusion is a commentary written by the author(s)/editor(s) that discusses the preceding text. Conclusions serve various purposes, among them summarizing and synthesizing important points of the material, emphasizing certain points for effect, providing a structural capstone to the text, driving home a particular point, or establishing extensions and generalizations for further consideration based upon the present document.

When formatting a conclusion for print publication, locate it after all other body matter but before all other back matter. Do not isolate the conclusion on a separate page from the material preceding it, unless it begins a separate chapter in a book-length work, in which case it should be headed with the word "Conclusion" coded as a chapter head (see section 4.12.1). When including a conclusion in an article-length text, format its title as an A-level subhead (see section 4.15). Material that follows the conclusion should be separated from it with a hard page break.

4.2.2 Appendixes

An appendix is a body of nonessential information that may be of interest to some readers but would be, if placed in the interior of the manuscript, more distracting than effective.

Appendixes vary significantly in terms of their content. Textual appendixes should be formatted as normal body text. Appendixes containing tables and other artwork should follow the guidelines for artwork in section 4.20. Generally, each appendix will be identified with a number or letter; its title (e.g., "Appendix 1" or "Appendix A") will be coded as a chapter head (see section 4.12.1); and it will usually be separated from other back matter with a hard page break or by being saved as a discrete computer file.

4.2.3 Notes

Notes are itemized ancillary commentary on isolated ideas or assertions in the body text. Notes are numbered—with superscripts or Arabic numerals in normal text size—in order to correspond to references—usually numerical superscripts—located at the relevant places in the body text. Notes placed at the bottom of the page are footnotes and should be formatted using the automatic footnoting feature of your word processor, if available; notes placed at the end of a text are known as endnotes. Unless specifically required to do otherwise, use endnotes, not footnotes.

Notes should be numbered sequentially throughout the manuscript. These numbers can begin at 1 in every new chapter if the notes are divided by chapter. See section 4.19 for how to treat in-text note references.

For endnotes in electronically submitted texts, double-space between each note, and do not indent any lines in a given paragraph (second and subsequent paragraphs may be indented). (Some styles, however, require notes to be indented five spaces using the tab key; follow such standards if required.) For print-only texts, double-space throughout (do not use an extra hard return between notes), and format note numbers using either regular Arabic numerals in normal text size or the superscript feature in your word processor.

If you are comfortable using a word processor's automatic footnote or endnote function, you should allow it to take care of formatting the notes for you in print-only texts; using a word processor's automatic footnote or endnote function can help ensure that in-text note numbers correspond with the notes themselves. Such automated features make corrections easier for the author but may be difficult for publishers to translate. Thus, in documents intended for publication, use manually formatted notes if there is any doubt about the publisher's translating abilities, even though this introduces the possibility that note numbers will lose their proper sequencing during revision. In electronically edited texts, some publishers place footnotes directly after the paragraphs in which the note references appear in order to avoid this problem. Follow publishers' guidelines scrupulously for manuscripts to be submitted from print publication.

4.2.4 Glossary

A glossary is an alphabetical listing of important terms used in the text. Italicize, underline, or tag (as appropriate) the term itself, and double-space the entries. For manuscripts to be submitted to publishers, separate each entry with a double hard return. Use the word "Glossary" coded as a chapter head (see section 4.12.1) at the top of the page, and separate the page from other back matter with a hard page break, or save the glossary as a discrete computer file.

4.2.5 Bibliography

A bibliography is a vertical list of information regarding works that were referenced in the creation of a manuscript. Forms and structures for organizing bibliographies vary significantly; however, the entries are almost always arranged alphabetically according to the last names of the cited author(s) or editor(s) or the first major word of the title for works where no author or editor is named.

For texts submitted electronically for print publication, double-space the entire bibliography, and do not indent any of the lines in the entry, unless required to do so. (Some styles require that the first line of each entry be indented five spaces or, using the tab key, one-half inch.) Separate each entry with two hard returns to create extra white space.

For work to be produced in hard copy only (such as most academic course papers), the most common format involves the use of hanging indentation, in which the first line of each entry is flush with the left margin while subsequent lines in the entry are indented five spaces or one-half inch. If you must follow such standards, use your word processor's automatic hanging indent function, if available; do not use hard returns and tab keys or change the margins to emulate the hanging indent.

For most styles, the bibliography for a shorter work (such as an article or essay) is placed on a separate page immediately following the body text. Format the title of the bibliography as a chapter head (see section 4.12.1), and separate the list from other back matter with a hard page break. The bibliography of a longer work may be saved as a separate computer file. Note that a bibliographic listing of the works directly referenced in a text is typically titled "Works Cited" or "References," while resources that were consulted but not cited while producing the manuscript are sometimes listed in a separate bibliography entitled "Works Consulted."

4.2.6 Index

An index is an alphabetical listing of topics, names, or titles discussed in the text. Each entry in the list is accompanied by a section or page number that tells the reader where to look in the text for corresponding information. For print-only texts, you may want to use the automatic indexing feature of your word processor if you are very familiar with it; however, for manuscripts to be submitted for print publication, it is generally better to format the index manually to avoid problems of translation. Indexes should usually be double-spaced throughout. Use the word "Index" coded as a chapter head at the top of the page (see section 4.12.1), and separate the index from other back matter by a hard page break; the index of a larger work may be saved as a discrete computer file. Do not format the index in columns or introduce other special features unless required to do so.

4.2.7 List of Contributors

The list of contributors presents brief biographical information about the authors who contributed to a text. Italicize, underline, or tag authors' names (as appropriate); double-space the biographies; and separate each entry with two hard returns. The list of contributors is generally only required for manuscripts being submitted for publication and should be saved as a separate computer file.

PRODUCING HARD-COPY DOCUMENTS ON A WORD PROCESSOR

4.3 Paper

Use only high-quality, clean, white, standard-sized paper (eight-and-a-half-inch by eleven-inch for North American standards; A4 for most others). Do not use erasable bond. Make sure you choose the appropriate paper for your printer type (i.e., laser or inkjet).

4.4 Printing

Use a good-quality printer. Laser print is the standard, but inkjet, daisy-wheel, and ribbon (dot matrix) are acceptable as long as the print is legible (for dot matrix, this usually means using the letter- or near-letter-quality setting on the printer). Be aware, however, that high-quality laser print on clean paper allows pages to be electronically scanned more easily, if this is a requirement. Print text in black only. Toner cartridges or ribbons must be refreshed if the print is faded, and you should clean the print heads following manufacturers' instructions. Print only on one side of the paper, and do not make any marks on the paper unless specifically required to do so.

4.5 Binding

Do not use store-bought covers to bind the pages of a paper unless specifically required to do so; instead, use a paper clip or a single staple in the upper left-hand corner. Plain envelopes (eight-and-a-half-inch by eleven-inch or A4, as appropriate) or folders can be used to protect a paper that is not handed directly to the recipient, but do not attach the paper to this packaging in any way. Follow guidelines for bylines and page numbers so that your manuscript can be kept in order.

4.6 Margins

Use one-inch margins on all four edges of the paper, unless specifically directed to do otherwise. (Some style guidelines or publishers' guidelines may require one-and-one-half-inch left-hand margins; oblige this request if necessary.) Header margins and footer margins, if used, should be set to one-half inch (the usual default setting in most word processors).

4.7 Spacing

Double-space the entire text, except when specifically required to do otherwise. Do not use extra hard returns to separate paragraphs, note entries, titles, or other textual elements unless specifically required to do so. For most styles, use two spaces after a period or a colon. (Some publishers may request that you use only one space after a period or colon; follow the specific guidelines for the style you are required to use.)

4.8 Fonts

Use a standard font such as Courier, Roman (or Times Roman, or Times New Roman), or Palatino (see figure 4.1). Twelve-point fonts are preferred, but ten point is also acceptable. Serif fonts (fonts with "tails," such as Courier and Roman) are generally easier to read than sans serif fonts (such as Arial or Helvetica) and are therefore generally preferred. Maintain the same font and font size throughout the text, except for footnote or endnote references, which are usually formatted in superscript, if possible. If you use the word processor's automatic note feature, you need not worry about changing fonts for note numbers. If you are required to format manually, eight-, nine-, or ten-point fonts, depending on the font size in the text, may be used to superscript footnote or endnote numbers. Some mathematical formulas may require super- or subscripting as well; font sizes may also be altered under those circumstances. Otherwise, do not change font size throughout the document.

4.9 Formatting Techniques

4.9.1 Boldface

Boldface is a formatting technique in which characters appear darker and thicker than normal text. Although it is widely used and misused by many authors and publishers for various reasons, it should be employed only in the rare circumstance of certain mathematical formulae that require it. Do not use it for emphasis

This is courier font

This is helvetica font

This is times font

This is times new roman

Figure 4.1 Common Fonts

or to format subheads, unless the specific style guide you must use requires it (some style guides require certain subheads to be bold-faced).

4.9.2 Underlining or Italics

Underlining and italics are formatting techniques used for emphasis or to set off special terminology in texts. Use one or the other, never both. Underlining is generally preferable to italics for documents to be submitted for print publication for the following reasons: (1) it is easier for readers and editors to identify in hard copy and onscreen, despite the improving qualities of printers and monitors; (2) authors often do not realize they have failed to italicize either the first or last letter of a word; (3) it is much easier for most publishers to translate from underlining to italics than to do the reverse (in publishing, in fact, underlining usually indicates text that should be italicized in final print copy). However, for documents to be produced as final copy (such as academic coursework) and for texts that will appear in electronic form, always use italics rather than underlining. Underlining is fast becoming a standard for denoting hypertext links and can therefore cause confusion.

Terminology

When an author refers to a particular word, phrase, or letter itself, such as in the statement "my definition of *honest* is . . . ," formatting is used to indicate such usage.

The preferred formatting for referenced terminology of this kind is either to underline or italicize the term as appropriate (following the guidelines in this section), although the use of quotation marks for the same effect (as in "honest" or 'honest') is widely practiced. Mathematical formulae, instructions, and computer code also should be treated as referenced terminology and therefore require special formatting, as should words and letters referred to as words and letters (as in "He misspelled the word by not including the silent *g*") and foreign words other than those found in a standard English dictionary (as in "She used the German word *Ewigweibliche*"). Some publishers may ask that terminology in electronic documents be enclosed within the <TEXT> ... </TEXT> tag pair, although the <TT> ... </TT> tag pair is preferable because it complies with the HTML standard. (See the discussion under corollary 3 in chapter 4 for more information on using tags for formatting discrete elements of a text.)

Emphasis

Underlining or italicizing (as appropriate) are the preferred methods in academic and scholarly writing for indicating textual emphasis, although boldface is widely misused for the same purpose. Some publishers may ask that emphasized text in electronic documents be enclosed within the <EM> ... </EM> tag pair. (See the discussion under corollary 3 in chapter 4 for more information on using tags for formatting discrete elements of a text.)

Title citations

A title citation is a reference to the actual name of a source text. Citations of titles of works of more substantial length, such as books, are either italicized or underlined as appropriate; in works submitted for print publication, titles may be enclosed within the <CITE> ... </CITE> tag pair. These tags eliminate the need to underline or italicize longer titles. Titles of shorter works, such as chapters, articles, essays, or poems, are typically enclosed in quotation marks (" ") in all formats.

4.10 Special Characters

Special characters are typographic symbols that do not appear on standard keyboards but are sometimes necessary when producing academic texts. The most commonly required special characters are accented characters such as ü, é, ç, ñ; mathematical symbols such as ±, ≥, Σ, and ∞; and typographical symbols such as £, ¶, §, and —. Most word processors can produce a variety of these symbols; consult the topics "special characters" or "character map" in a software manual or through the online help function of your word processor to locate information on how to handle special characters.

There are, however, standards for special characters. The most widely used standard is currently the ISO Latin-1 character set, which assigns a particular code to 256 common characters. Some may be more familiar with the ASCII character set, which is actually a subset of ISO Latin-1: it comprises the first 128 characters of the ISO set. For example, the code for the ~ symbol in both ISO and ASCII is 126. The ISO Latin-1 set is printed in the appendix.

Special characters may need to be inserted by hand on printed copies. On disks to be submitted for publication, you may need to designate special characters with an asterisk or other symbol if your word processor cannot handle them. Consult your publisher if in doubt.

4.11 Bylines

A byline indicates the author(s) of the work and other relevant information such as affiliation or geographic location. For article- or chapter-length texts, it should be placed flush left at the top, left-hand corner of the first page, above the title of the work but below the page number and header. Bylines placed on cover pages typically follow the title. List each author's first name followed by the middle initial and surname. On a separate line or lines include other relevant information, such as date, course number, and/or institutional affiliation. Double-space the text in the byline, and use the same font that appears in the body of the manuscript. Do not include a byline when submitting work for anonymous grading or review.

4.12 Titles

A title is the name given to a work by an author. Academic works tend to feature titles that reflect the focus of the manuscript. Titles also indicate division and subordination of ideas. For example, book titles describe the general purpose of a large manuscript, and chapter titles describe ideas contained in smaller units that, in turn, form the work as a whole.

4.12.1 Titles for Article- or Chapter-Length Projects

Place the title below the byline on the first page of the article or essay, separating it from the byline and the body of the work by one double-space in humanities styles. In scientific styles requiring a cover page, place the title at the top of the cover page, followed by the byline. In hard-copy-only texts, titles for shorter works require no formatting; however, in texts submitted on disk for print publication, such titles should be enclosed within the <H2> . . . </H2> tag pair and separated from following text by an extra line space (i.e., a double hard return). Set titles in upper- and lowercase letters—never use all capital letters—and do not boldface, underline, or italicize them. Center titles on the line for print-only formats, using the automatic centering feature of your word processor; do not change margins or use the space bar or the tab key to center titles. (See figure 4.2 on page 139.)

4.12.2 Titles for Book-Length Projects

In the case of book-length projects (approximately twenty-five thousand or more words), the title of the work should be placed at the top of the title page, beneath the top margin. In print-only texts, these titles should be either italicized or underlined, as appropriate (see section 4.9.2); do not use boldface or all capital letters. In texts for print publication, instead of underlining or boldfacing the title, enclose it within the <H1> ... </H1> tag pair.

4.13 Section or Page Numbers

Section numbers and page numbers provide a constant and sequential system for referencing specific locations in a text. Use your word processor's automatic page numbering function to place the page numbers in the top, right-hand corner of the manuscript (in most cases, in the header, following the author's last name or the running head). Unless you are very comfortable using a word processor's automatic paragraph numbering functions, however, manually insert section numbers in the appropriate places, leaving an extra line space before the number. Do not include any other text on the same line with a section number. Number every page of your text, including the first, unless required otherwise.

4.14 Headers and Footers

Headers and footers are elements that appear on every page of a manuscript in either the top or bottom margin. They typically contain page numbers and the author's last name or a shortened version of the document title (called a "running head").

Headers and footers should be inserted using the automated formatting function available on your word processor. Headers are one of the few elements that should be justified flush right (against the right-hand margin); footers should usually be centered. Headers and footers should be formatted to appear approximately at the midpoint of either the top or bottom margin (about a half inch from the top or bottom of the page). Headers and footers should contain only the last name of the author (the name of the first author in the case of a collaborative text) and a page number, unless the manuscript is supposed to be anonymous or you are required to do otherwise by the style guide you are following. In the case of anonymous submissions, headers and footers should contain a running head. Note that book-length titles in headers and footers must still be italicized or underlined as appropriate (see section 4.9.2). The text in a header or footer should be followed by a single space and then the page number. No dashes or abbreviations such as *pg.* are required to separate the text in a header or footer from page numbers.

4.15 Subheads

Subheads are titles that give structure to the text by differentiating among its various segments. Subheads are subordinate to the title of the work itself or the title of the chapter in which they appear. Subheads may appear within segments already set off by subheads, much as subtopics may fall within other subtopics in an outline. Like subtopics in an outline, the level of subordination of subheads is indicated by formatting. But whereas in outlines indentation communicates which topics are subtopics of which, each style manual formats text subheads differently. You should follow the guidelines of the particular manual you are honoring. What is most important is that you format subheads consistently: all A-level subheads should be formatted the same, all B-level subheads the same, and so on.

In texts that will appear only as hard copy, we recommend that subheads be formatted as follows (see also figure 4.2):

A-level subhead: Upper- and lowercase letters, flush with left-hand margin, and separated from preceding text by a double hard return and from following text by a single hard return.

B-level subhead: Italicized upper- and lowercase letters, set flush with the left-hand margin, separated from preceding text with a double hard return and from following text with a single hard return.

C-level subhead: Italicized or underlined as appropriate (see section 4.9.2), set flush with the left-hand margin, ending with a period, and separated from the preceding text with a double hard return. Subsequent text should be run in. Uppercase only the first letter and any proper nouns.

D-level subhead: Indent five spaces or one-half inch from the left-hand margin, uppercasing only the first letter and any proper nouns. Italicize or underline as appropriate, end with a period, and run in subsequent text. Precede paragraphs beginning with D-level subheads with a single hard return, as you would any new paragraph.

In texts prepared for submission on disk, set all subheads on lines of their own, flush with the left-hand margin. Do not precede or follow them with extra line spaces. Always use upper- and lowercase letters, not all capitals. Do not use boldface, italics, underlining, or centering to format subheads. Instead, they should be formatted using the following tag pairs:

<H3>[A-level subhead]</H3>

<H4>[B-level subhead]</H4>

<H5>[C-level subhead]</H5>

<H6>[D-level subhead]</H6>

Note that the <H1> . . . </H1> tag pair is reserved for book titles and the <H2> . . . </H2> tag pair is for chapter or article titles.

4.16 Paragraphs

A paragraph is a group of consecutive sentences, each of which relates to a single idea; sentences within each paragraph are grouped together and set apart from other paragraphs in order to provide thematic and textual structure.

The first paragraph of a text or subsection (i.e., paragraphs immediately following subheads or space breaks) requires no indentation. Otherwise, when formatting paragraphs for a document

Janice R. Walker

Professor Taylor

English 6700

8 January, 1998

Paper or Chapter Title

Formatting Paper Titles: Works Composed for Print

In texts that will appear only as hard copy, we recommend that paper titles be centered, using upper- and lowercase letters. The title should be separated from other text by a single hard-return.

Walker 2

Many short titles use only the main title. However, sometimes sub-headings are used to aid the reader.

Format of A-Level Subheads

A-level subheads should be separated from the preceding text by an extra hard return. Use upper- and lowercase letters.

A-level subhead

Walker 3

For texts which require additional levels of subheads, we recommend the following formats.

Format of B-Level Subheads

Use upper- and lowercase letters, italicized or underlined (as appropriate). Separate from preceding text with an extra hard return.

B-level subhead

Walker 4

Additional subheads can also be used if necessary.

Formatting of additional subheads. For C-level subheads, capitalize the first word and any proper nouns only; italicize or underline (as appropriate); end the subhead with a period and continue the body text on the same line.

C-level subheads

Walker 5

Separate D-level subheads from preceding text with only a single hard return.

Formatting of D-level subheads. Indent five spaces or one-half inch from the left-hand margin. Use uppercase only for the first letter and any proper nouns in the subhead, italicize (or underline if appropriate) the text and conclude with a period. The following text continues on the same line.

D-level subheads

Figure 4.2 Subhead Formats for Printed Texts

that will be printed, indent the first line of each new paragraph with a tab and conclude each paragraph with a single hard return. Do not use the space bar to indent new paragraphs. And do not rely on an automatic (soft) return to conclude a paragraph.

4.17 Lists

4.17.1 Ordered Lists

An ordered list is a vertical list of textual items that have a logical sequence, with this sequence indicated not only by ordering the items appropriately but also by preceding each item with a sequential number or letter.

Ordered lists should be arranged vertically, with each item beginning on a new line. Ordered lists should also be arranged hierarchically or chronologically. Depending on the context, each item in the list should be preceded by either an ascending or descending number or letter, although numbers are generally preferred to letters, and ascending order is generally preferred to descending.

Ordered lists in print-only texts should be indented using a double tab (about ten spaces) to set them off from normal body text. If you are very comfortable with a word processor's automatic function for creating ordered lists, you should use it. Otherwise, use the word processor's indent function to change the margins for the text in a numbered list. Do not place an extra line space before the first item or after the last item on the list. Place a period after each number, skip one space, and then begin the text. See figure 4.3 for an example of an ordered list in a print-only text.

In texts submitted in electronic form for print publication, ordered lists should be set off from normal body text by the inclusion of an <OL> tag in front of the entire list and an </OL> tag at the end. Do not indent the list, and do not precede or follow it with an extra line space. Each item in the list should be enclosed with the <LI>. . . </LI> tag pair and flush with the left-hand margin. Do not use your word processor's automated function for numbering

An ordered list

Indent each item in the list
10 spaces.

Follow each item with a
single hard-return.

> Walker 5
>
> Ordered lists should be arranged vertically, with each item beginning on a new line. Depending on the context, each item on the list should be preceded by either an ascending or descending number or.
>
> 1. Woke up
> 2. Took a shower
> 3. Went to work
> 4. Ate lunch
> 5. Went home
>
> Ordered lists in print-only texts should be indented ten spaces to set them off from normal body text.

One space after the period or
bullet.

Do not skip extra lines before
or after a list.

An unordered list

> Walker 6
>
> Unordered lists should be arranged vertically, with each item beginning on a new line.
>
> • Dogs
> • Cats
> • Fish
> • Birds
> • Snakes
>
> Consult your word processor's help function or manual under the topics "bullets" or "special characters" for help inserting bullets. Do not precede or follow the list with an extra line space. Place a single space afer the bullet, and then begin the text.

Figure 4.3 List Formats in Printed Texts

lists, unless you are certain that your publisher will accept such formatting. See figure 4.4 for an example of an ordered list in an electronic/print text.

4.17.2 Unordered Lists

An unordered list is a vertical list of textual items that have no significant logical sequence. Unordered lists are typically bulleted.

Unordered lists should be arranged vertically, with each item beginning on a new line. Unordered lists are not hierarchical or chronological; each item on the list is more or less as important as

An ordered list in a manuscript submitted to a publisher

Walker 7

In texts to be submitted for print publication, ordered lists should be set off from normal body text with tags.

```
<OL>
<LI>Woke up</LI>
<LI>Took a shower</LI>
<LI>Went to work</LI>
<LI>Ate lunch</LI>
<LI>Went home</LI>
</OL>
```

Do not indent the list, and do not precede or follow it with an extra line space.

An unordered list in a manuscript submitted to a publisher

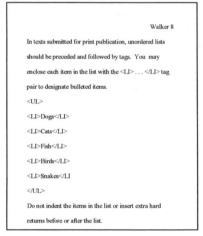

Walker 8

In texts submitted for print publication, unordered lists should be preceded and followed by tags. You may enclose each item in the list with the <LI> . . . </LI> tag pair to designate bulleted items.

```
<UL>
<LI>Dogs</LI>
<LI>Cats</LI>
<LI>Fish</LI>
<LI>Birds</LI>
<LI>Snakes</LI
</UL>
```

Do not indent the items in the list or insert extra hard returns before or after the list.

Figure 4.4 List Formats in Manuscripts Submitted for Publication

any other item on the list. Consequently, unordered lists are bulleted, whereas ordered lists have numbers or letters that reflect the assigned order. Consult your word processor's help function or manual under the topics "bullets" or "special characters" for help inserting bullets. Do not precede or follow the list with an extra line space. Place a single space after the bullet, and then begin the text. You may use your word processor's automated bulleting function if you are comfortable with it and certain that your publisher allows it, or you may chose to format unordered lists manually (see figure 4.3). In texts submitted for print publication, place a <UL> tag at the beginning of an unordered list and a </UL> tag at the end of it (see figure 4.4). Each item in the list should be enclosed with the <LI> . . . </LI> tag pair and flush with the left-hand margin; do not indent.

4.18 Quotations

4.18.1 Block Quotations

Block quotations are quotations of roughly forty words or more that are indented more than normal body text. In professional publications, block quotations are sometimes printed in a smaller or different font from normal body text.

In print-only texts, the preferred format for block quotations is to indent the quotation ten spaces from the left margin (use your word processor's paragraph-indent capability to do this; never use the tab key or space bar for this purpose), leaving the right margin exactly the same as normal body text. The quotation should be double-spaced throughout, and you need not insert an extra line space before or after it. Block quotations should never be enclosed with quotation marks.

In preparing texts for print publication, begin a block quote with a <BLOCKQUOTE> tag, followed by a </BLOCKQUOTE> tag. Double-space it throughout, and do not set it off with extra line spaces or enclose it within quotation marks. Do not indent the first line of the quotation.

4.18.2 Epigraphs

Epigraphs are quotations placed at the very beginning of a text that somehow reflect a central idea in the text. They tend to be especially provocative or well worded.

Epigraphs should be used sparingly. In print-only texts, they should be indented ten spaces from the left margin (use your word processor's automatic paragraph-indent function to do this) and separated from the title above and the first paragraph of the text below by two hard returns. Place the author's name and the title of the excerpted work on a separate line from the quotation itself. These elements may be placed flush right or indented further.

In electronic texts submitted for print publication, use the <BLOCKQUOTE> . . . </BLOCKQUOTE> tag pair to format epigraphs like block quotations. The author's name and the title of the excerpted work should appear on a separate line, and the concluding </BLOCKQUOTE> tag should follow the title. All text should be typed flush with the left-hand margin; do not indent.

4.19 Note References

Numbers are sometimes placed in the body text, usually at the ends of sentences, to direct the reader to notes located at the bottoms of the pages, at the end of the document, or at the end of a subsection of the document. Corresponding numbers are placed in front of each note.

Note numbers are generally formatted in superscript, which means they hang slightly above the line on which normal body text is printed. Note numbers can be set in either eight-, nine-, or ten-point font if necessary (some word processors and printers will cut off the tops of superscript numbers unless they are reduced), or you may keep them the same size as the body text if you prefer. See section 4.2.3 for information on where to locate notes and how to format them.

4.20 Artwork

In the context of publishing, "artwork" refers to any element in a manuscript that is not textual. This includes tables, illustrations, figures, graphics, and photographs. Each individual piece of artwork should generally be stored apart from the rest of the manuscript on separate pages and as separate computer files.

Authors should be especially careful when using artwork. They should be certain that copyright has not been violated and that the artwork is appropriate and of sufficient quality to be reproduced effectively if necessary.

4.20.1 Tables

A table is an arrangement of words, letters, or numbers in the form of a grid or a matrix (although the lines of the grid or matrix may not be visible). Tables are designed to be read horizontally across columns and vertically down rows.

Simple tables may be created with tabs (never the space bar) to format columns and hard returns to format rows, or you may use your word processor's automatic table or columns feature if you are familiar with it and your publisher can handle it. Tables may be prepared on separate pages or placed in the interior of a manuscript, alongside normal text. When formatting tables, avoid using any formatting feature other than underlining or italics as appropriate (see section 4.9.2); that is, do not center or justify text; do not change fonts; do not use boldfaced type.

More complex tables need special attention. Even though increasingly more word processors offer automated functions for creating tables, authors should not use these functions to place tables in the interior of a text unless they are very comfortable with these features and publishers' guidelines specifically allow them. Instead, for manuscripts to be submitted to publishers, complex tables should be placed on separate sheets or leafs. Authors may use the automated functions of word processing or spreadsheet software to help generate such tables, but they should be stored as computer files independent from the rest of the manuscript, to be physically inserted as separate pages when the final copy is submitted. The text must make clear references to the names of any tables at the appropriate places, and each table must be labeled clearly, formatted cleanly, and printed neatly.

4.20.2 Illustrations

Illustrations are drawings. For texts prepared for submission to publishers, they should be placed on pages separate from the text and, if stored electronically, saved in a separate file. For all types of manuscripts, the text itself must make clear reference to each illustration at the appropriate place, and the illustrations must be labeled clearly, formatted cleanly, and printed neatly.

4.20.3 Figures

Figures are illustrations that include text. Graphs and charts are some of the most common figures.

For works to be submitted to publishers, figures should be placed on pages separate from the text or, if stored electronically, saved in a separate file. The text itself must make clear reference to each figure at the appropriate place, and the figures must be labeled clearly, formatted cleanly, and printed neatly.

Even though increasingly more word processors offer automated functions for creating graphs and charts, authors should not use these functions to place such figures in the interior of texts intended for submission to publishers unless they are specifically allowed and only when they have truly mastered the requirements for inserting such artwork. Authors may use the automated functions of word processing, spreadsheet, or graphics software to help generate charts or graphs, but such figures should still be stored as files independent from the rest of the manuscript, to be physically inserted as separate pages when final copy is submitted.

4.20.4 Graphics

Although a graphic is technically any piece of artwork, the term is most often associated with illustrations that make particular use of shading, color, and contrast for effect. Ruler lines and other minimal markings used throughout a text are also considered graphics.

Ruler lines (horizontal lines drawn across a page to enhance readability) are just about the only graphic that most authors will need to consider. Avoid using such graphics unless absolutely necessary. If you must create a ruler line in an electronic text to be submitted for print publication, use either the hyphen key or the underlining key (shift-hyphen) rather than any automated word-processing function that provides ruler lines. For print-only texts, you may, of course, use the automated features provided in your word processor.

4.20.5 Photographs

A photograph is a picture taken with a camera. In document production, photographs often must be scanned to produce separations (of color pictures) or halftones (of black-and-white pictures) so that they will reproduce vividly on paper.

For manuscripts to be submitted to publishers, photographs should be placed on pages separate from the text or, if stored electronically, saved in a separate file. In all cases, the text itself must make clear reference to each photograph at the appropriate place, and the photographs must be labeled clearly and, if necessary, reproduced cleanly. Some photocopiers now have settings for copying photographs; use such settings if available.

Even though increasingly more word processors offer automated functions for importing images, authors preparing texts for submission to publishers should not use these functions to place photographs in the interior of a text unless they are thoroughly familiar with this feature and the publisher specifically allows it. Authors should feel welcome, however, to use technologies such as digital cameras and software that help manipulate and print photographic images, but the resulting digital photographs should still be stored as files independent from the rest of the manuscript, to be physically inserted as separate pages when final copy is submitted to publishers.

PREPARING DISKETTES

Use high-quality, three-and-a-half-inch, high-density diskettes (IBM is the standard format). Label diskettes clearly, including the name, phone number, and email address of a person to contact in the event of problems. Be sure to write legibly on the diskette label, not on the diskette itself.

4.21 Naming Computer Files

Use no more than eight characters for the prefix and three characters for the file extension to ensure compatibility. Do not include spaces in the file names; instead, use the underscore character (_) if you need to designate a space. For nonanonymous submissions of work on a diskette or other electronic medium, use a version of the author's last name followed by a file extension that indicates the file format in which the text was saved (the default file extension is appropriate for most computer applications). For example, taylor.txt would be ASCII format; taylor.wpd would be WordPerfect 6.0 or above; taylor.doc would be used for earlier versions of WordPerfect files or for Word files; taylor.htm would be HTML format. Using the proper file extension will allow most computer applications to recognize the type of file automatically and translate it accurately.

If multiple files are submitted (including illustrations, figures, and so on, or for multiple sections or chapters saved as separate files), number the files sequentially and indicate the file format. For example, tay_fig1.gif (figure 1 of the Taylor manuscript, in GIF format), tay_fig2.jpg (figure 2 of the Taylor manuscript, in JPEG format), tay_ch1.txt (chapter 1 of the Taylor manuscript, in ASCII format), or tay_ch2.wpd (chapter 2 of the Taylor manuscript, in WordPerfect 8.0 format).

If different parts of a manuscript are saved as separate files, file names should reflect both the author's name and the name of the individual element. For example, tay_pre.txt (preface of the Taylor manuscript, in ASCII format) or tay_toc.doc (table of contents of the Taylor manuscript, in Word format). For a complex manuscript submission with many files, diskettes should be accompanied by a typewritten, annotated explanation of the contents and format of each file. For smaller submissions, list the file names and each file's type on the diskette label.

If the name of the author must be kept anonymous for review purposes, follow the principles outlined above, only substitute the first important word (or a truncated version) of the title for the author's name. For example, if an article entitled "The Changing Internet" were being submitted, it should be named changing.txt, changing.wpd, changing.doc, or changing.htm (as appropriate), and auxiliary files of the article or manuscript should be titled cha_fig1.gif or cha_fig2.jpg or the like.

4.22 Sending Diskettes Through the Mail

Place diskettes sent through the mail in a protective sleeve or envelope. Homemade cardboard sleeves are often as effective as store-bought ones and much less expensive. Be sure no tape, adhesive, or staples touch the diskette, and protect diskettes from exposure to excessive heat or cold or to magnetization by clearly indicating the contents on the exterior of the envelope.

5

Network Format

This chapter presents effective standards and guidelines for authors, editors, and publishers who wish to create electronic documents that are easily transferable from one application or platform to another, especially if these texts are to be published on computer networks, such as the WWW. Authors whose work will be published on a computer network, such as the World Wide Web, should follow the standards described in this chapter. This chapter is not intended to itemize all the ins and outs of HTML coding; for that, you should buy one of the many guides already in print or visit the NCSA's *Beginner's Guide to HTML* online.

The logic of computer networks can contribute immensely to developing standards for academic document format online. In order for computer files to be exchanged across platforms and applications, these files must be prepared using generic formats so that a variety of people using a variety of computer equipment and software can gain access. As a result, highly uniform format standards, such as HTML, have begun to emerge. As with documents intended for print formats, however, a cardinal rule governs working with documents intended for electronic publication: *In all circumstances, keep it simple.*

The guidelines in this chapter are intended to prevent the unique logic of a word processor from interfering with the easy portability of files to a network. Many authors of academic texts are likely to use a word-processing program to compose and format documents for electronic publication. Many of the newer versions of most word processors allow for automatic translation of standard word-processing codes into HTML format. Translating many of the automatic formatting features of a word processor can still cause problems, however, so avoid using these features (such as the automatic paragraph indent or automatic footnoting features) if possible. If you are using the automatic HTML publishing feature of a word processor, avoid including hypertextual tags (i.e., tags enclosed in angle brackets) in the text: angle brackets are reserved characters in hypertext, yet most word processors will automatically translate them into codes rather than retaining them as hypertext commands. Instead, you will need to add these commands to the hypertext using an ASCII text editor or HTML editor in order to format your document adequately. Use a Web browser to verify that any documents you translate from a word processor to HTML format have been formatted properly.

The cardinal rule of online document design has three important corollaries:

Corollary 1: Do not use any of your text editor's formatting features unless you absolutely must. Do not change fonts, do not change margins, do not use fancy fonts, do not center or fully justify text, do not use blinking text unless you absolutely must in order to meet the demands of your intended audience.

Corollary 2: Do not invent new elements of document style unless you absolutely must. Almost all professional academic authors will need only two special formatting features to produce an online text: italics (not underlining) and hypertextual links (see section 5.5). Authors who wish to use footnotes or endnotes should consider using hypertextual links. Authors working online must also abjure hanging indentation for bibliographic entries because most HTML documents do not readily lend themselves to this formatting. All authors should, however, take advantage of text-editor functions such as spell checkers.

Corollary 3: Use logical tags, not typographical formatting, to denote the various elements of document style. These tags can easily be replaced by either traditional word-processing commands or HTML tags, as necessary. See the discussion under Corollary 3 in chapter 4 for an explanation of the logic behind these formatting codes.

✳ ✳ ✳

Keeping the cardinal rule of document design for networked texts and its three corollaries in mind can solve a great many problems for authors, editors, and publishers; however, specific ramifications of these rules need to be spelled out. Table 5.1 summarizes the general rules to follow when preparing a document for electronic publication. More detailed explanations and rules for the individual components of document style follow.

THE PARTS OF THE TEXT

5.1 Front Matter

See section 4.1. Front matter of chapter- and article-length texts may be stored in the same file and at the same URL as the body text; however, the author may want to use page anchor tags (see section 5.4) to allow navigation around the various elements of the text. Each element of front matter for longer projects should be stored in a separate computer file, located at a unique URL. In such cases, authors should provide navigational links to identify and access such information.

Authors working in HTML/SGML or other similar formats should use metatags on each separate file. Metatags are hypertext tags within the <HEAD> . . . </HEAD> tag pair of an HTML file that provide information about the document, such as the au-

TABLE 5.1

- Use metatags to identify authors, contributors, titles, and necessary publication information.

- Be aware that some formatting features will not be readable by all Web browsers; you should therefore try to use only the basic formatting features and codes described in this chapter unless you are absolutely required to do otherwise.

- Avoid using underlining for most purposes; use italics instead.

- Use boldface sparingly—for instance, when required in certain mathematical formulas.

- Use the paragraph tags (<P> and </P>) to separate sections and paragraphs preceded and followed by extra line space. See section 5.16 for a discussion of these tags.

- Do not use the space bar or tab key to indent. Paragraphs should be set off with the paragraph tags; they need not be indented. Block quotations, lists, and other elements that may require indenting in final electronically published form should be set off using the proper HTML tags (e.g., <BLOCKQUOTE>... </BLOCKQUOTE>, <OL>...</OL>, and <UL>...</UL>).

- In most instances, allow lines to wrap automatically; do not try to force features of print texts, such as double spacing and hanging indents, into electronic formats, as these features may create difficulty for some readers using different hardware and software applications.

- Use the line break tag (<BR>) as necessary to force a line break without adding an extra line space, for example, preceding lists.

- Use the table codes to create simple tables.

- Do not center or right-justify text unless absolutely required to do so. If you must center some portions of your text, use the <CENTER> ... </CENTER> tag pair or other appropriate HTML coding.

- For most academic texts, keep your design relatively austere. These texts need to be especially portable and readable, and advanced formatting codes and applications (such as large graphics files or audio and video files requiring plug-ins or special browsers) may prevent many readers with limited technological capabilities from accessing your work.

- Format your documents carefully to save potential readers, compilers, and editors anguish. Each online document should contain a byline and a title (see sections 5.11 and 5.12). If your document contains multiple files, it should contain a title or contents page to which all other pages in the work refer (see sections 5.1.2 and 5.1.5).

thor's name, the creation date, title, and description of the document. This information can then be sought using search engines designed for the purpose; it can also be accessed by viewing the file's HTML source code. For example, the following code will allow the information contained in it to be viewed in the source code and indexed by search engines and other programs that search for specific information online:

<META NAME= "Author" CONTENT= "Janice Walker">

<META NAME= "Creation Date" CONTENT= "21 Jun. 1998 15:54 GMT">

<META NAME= "Title" CONTENT= "Metatags">

<META NAME= "Abstract" CONTENT= "Examples of the use of metatags to provide bibliographic information in hypertext documents">

Metatags can also contain other information, such as keywords chosen by the author to facilitate searches. Many HTML editing programs will automatically include some of this information.

The following elements are discussed in the order in which they usually appear in texts.

5.1.1 Covers and Cover Pages

Cover

Material relating to the cover, if applicable, should be stored in a separate file and at a different URL from the rest of the publication, often the index.html page (see section 5.3). Covers for online publications should contain obvious links to the rest of the text.

Cover page

A cover page is a single page that contains at least the complete title of the work and the name(s) and affiliation(s) of the work's author(s), editor(s), and translator(s). Articles, essays, and chapters do not necessarily require cover pages; the title, the authors' names and affiliations, and the date of publication can be placed on the first page of the text instead. If used, however, the cover page should be located at a discrete URL and should thus contain an obvious link (or links) to the rest of the text.

5.1.2 Title Page

See section 4.1.2. The title page should also list the URL of publication and may include the email addresses of the author(s) or editor(s) and the publication date. Other appropriate information (such as any special software applications necessary to access the text adequately) may also be included.

5.1.3 Information Page

See section 4.1.3. Note that the appropriateness of including some of this information online is questionable.

5.1.4 Abstract or Summary

See section 4.1.4. When formatting an abstract, locate it either immediately after the title of the publication or at a separate URL.

Head it with the word "Abstract" enclosed within the <H2> . . . </H2> tag pair to designate it as a chapter head (see section 4.12.1). Note: In hypertext documents, it is not necessary to center titles or subheads unless you prefer to do so.

5.1.5 Table of Contents

The table of contents is a list of the major divisions, sections, or chapters of a book-length manuscript. Because page numbers are irrelevant online, the contents should use hypertextual links rather than page numbers to key the names of the major divisions to the relevant subsections (see section 5.5). Head the contents with the words "Table of Contents" (or "Contents") coded as a chapter head (i.e., enclosed within the <H2> . . . </H2> tag pair; see section 4.12.1).

5.1.6 List of Illustrations and Figures

See section 4.1.6. Because page numbers are irrelevant online, the list may contain hypertextual links between the items noted and the corresponding artwork rather than page numbers (see section 5.5). Code the title of the page or section as a chapter head by enclosing it within the <H2> . . . </H2> tag pair (see section 4.12.1).

5.1.7 List of Tables

See section 4.1.7. Each title in such a list should be a hypertextual link to the appropriate table or page online (see section 5.5). Code the title of the page or section as a chapter head by enclosing it within the <H2> . . . </H2> tag pair (see section 4.12.1).

5.1.8 Foreword

See section 4.1.8. In a longer text, the foreword should be placed in a separate file with a unique URL. Code the title of the page or section as a chapter head by enclosing it within the <H2> . . . </H2> tag pair (see section 4.12.1).

5.1.9 Acknowledgments

See section 4.1.9. In a longer text, the acknowledgments should be placed in a separate file with a unique URL, unless they are included in the preface, which is often the case. Code the title of the page or section as a chapter head by enclosing it within the <H2> . . . </H2> tag pair (see section 4.12.1).

5.1.10 Preface

A preface is a commentary written by the author(s) that discusses the project that follows. Prefaces typically address information about the publication of the text, such as the history of the project, important contributors, or editions or translations of the text; such information may also be handled through an author's or editor's note.

When formatting a preface for a book-length electronic publication, head the text with the word "Preface" coded as a chapter head (i.e., enclosed within the <H2> . . . </H2> tag pair; see section 4.12.1). When including a preface in an article-length text, format its title as an A-level subhead (see section 4.15); do not place the preface on a separate page from the material that follows, unless it is longer than two thousand words.

5.1.11 Introduction

An introduction is commentary written by the author(s) that discusses the project that follows. Unlike a preface, introductions typically orient the reader to the ensuing text's argument or content, usually including substantial information about the organization and theme of the text. However, no hard-and-fast rule can be said to distinguish clearly the function of a preface from that of an introduction. It is highly unlikely that an article will require both a preface and an introduction, although this is not uncommon in book-length works.

When formatting an introduction for a publication, locate it immediately before the body of the text, but do not place it on a separate page unless it is longer than about two thousand words. In a book-length text, title it with the word "Introduction" coded as a chapter head with the <H2> . . . </H2> tag pair (see section 4.12.1); in an article-length text, format the title as an A-level subhead (see section 4.15).

5.2 Back Matter

See section 4.2. Whenever placing an item of back matter at a separate URL instead of at the same URL as the body text, authors must provide navigational links to identify and access such information.

5.2.1 Conclusion

A conclusion is a commentary written by the author(s)/editor(s) that discusses the preceding text. Conclusions serve various purposes, among them summarizing and synthesizing important points of the material, emphasizing certain points for effect, providing a structural capstone to the text, driving home a particular point, or establishing extensions and generalizations for further consideration based upon the present document.

When formatting a conclusion for electronic publication, locate it after all other body matter but before all other back matter. Do not isolate the conclusion on a separate page, unless it is longer than about two thousand words. In a book-length text, title it with the word "Conclusion" coded as a chapter head with the <H2> . . . </H2> tag pair (see section 4.12.1); in an article-length text, format the title as an A level subhead (see section 4.15).

5.2.2 Appendixes

See section 4.2.2. Follow the guidelines for artwork in section 5.20, including all the subsections there, for appendixes containing tables and other artwork.

5.2.3 Notes

Notes are itemized ancillary commentary on isolated ideas or assertions in the body text. Notes are generally numbered in order to correspond to references—usually numerical superscripts—located at the relevant places in the body text. Locate the notes themselves at the end of the document, before the bibliography, and entitle them with the word "Notes" coded as a chapter head with the <H2> ... </H2> tag pair (see section 4.12.1). Superscript note references are often difficult to read online, thus, if you prefer, use hypertextual links instead to connect paraphrasings or quotations to their sources, in which case you may choose to locate the notes at a separate URL (see section 5.5). Hypertextual links between citations in the body text itself and the bibliography can also be highly effective. However, most academic hypertext should follow traditional parenthetical citation formats. Even there, though, references to other online sources should also be linked to the original source if possible. For a more complete discussion of in-text citations, see chapter 2.

5.2.4 Glossary

A glossary is an alphabetical listing of important terms used in the text. For hypertext glossaries, enclose the entire list within the <DL> ... </DL> tag pair; precede each term with the <DT> tag and each definition with the <DD> tag. Code the title of the page or section (i.e., "Glossary") as a chapter head using the <H2> ... </H2> tag pair (see section 4.12.1). Creating hypertextual links between in-text terms and glossary entries is an especially effective way to format a glossary (see section 5.5).

5.2.5 Bibliography

A bibliography is a list of information regarding works that were referenced in the creation of a manuscript. Eventually, lists of sources may be unnecessary, if the cited texts themselves are hypertext links to the original sources. When a document is likely to be printed out, however, parenthetical references to the text will continue to be necessary. Because hypertext links do not necessarily show the URL when they are printed out, for now the bibliography is a necessity in any text—especially an academic text—that refers to outside sources, even if all those sources are located online.

Forms and structures for organizing bibliographies vary significantly; however, the entries are almost always arranged alphabetically according to the last names of the cited author(s) or editor(s) or the first major word in the title of the work being cited if no author or editor name is available. A bibliographic listing of the works directly referenced in a text is typically titled "Works Cited" or "References." Resources that were consulted but not cited while producing the manuscript are sometimes listed in a separate bibliography entitled "Works Consulted." Whatever the title chosen, code it as a chapter head by enclosing it within the <H2> ... </H2> tag pair (see section 4.12.1).

The bibliography should be located at the end of a document. Surround each entry in a bibliography with paragraph tags (<P> and </P>; see section 5.16) so it will be followed by white space. No indentation is necessary. You may also arrange an online bibliography as an unordered list. Place the <UL> tag in front of the entire bibliography and the </UL> tag at the end. Place an <LI> tag (used to code a bulleted list) in front of each entry (see sections 5.17.1. and 5.17.2, as well as figure 5.1, which provides an example of a bulleted list used for a bibliography) or use the <P> ... </P> tag pair instead (this will prevent bullets from appearing in front of each item and separate each entry from the next with white space). Do *not* try to form hanging indents online as this may interfere with the automatic word-wrap feature in most browsers and cause difficulty for the reader.

> • Haile, Mitchell. "Research and Reference Starting Links." Vers. 2.0.
> Rev. 22 Jun. 1996. http://www.nyx.net/~jhaile/net/research.html (3 Aug.
> 1996).
>
> • herb (#198). "Insectia Tribune (#1300)." *DaMOO*.
> telnet://lrc.csun.edu:7777 read #1300 (11 Aug. 1996).

Figure 5.1 An Example of a Bulleted List Used for References

If you make use of hypertextual links (see section 5.5), you can place the bibliography at a separate URL. Hypertextual links between citations in the body text itself and a bibliography can be highly effective. (For example, in figure 5.2 the underlined references in the text point to the reference in the bibliography, and the entry in the bibliography in figure 5.1 points to the source itself.) Parenthetical references will still be necessary, however, for most academic texts. Full URLs should be listed for each online source, as well, even if an entry is already linked to its source; this will ensure that readers will be able to obtain access to the sources even if they are unable to follow the links (as may occur if the hypertext has been printed out).

5.2.6 Index

An index is an alphabetical listing of topics, names, or titles discussed in the text. Because page numbers do not really exist in online documents, indexes should use hypertextual links between entries in the index and the referenced text (see section 5.5). However, because each entry may need to link to more than one location, online indexes may be very difficult to format. Moreover, because electronic text can be more easily searched than print text, indexes may be less necessary. Even so, a list of key terms with links to the corresponding chapters or URLs discussing such terms can be helpful to readers. Once inside a particular URL, a reader can search for the indexed word itself. If an indexed word is a common term or appears repeatedly throughout a text, authors can cite it as part of the relevant phrase in which it appears in the body text so that readers can search for the reference more precisely.

If included, the index page should be headed with the word "Index" coded as a chapter head using the <H2> . . . </H2> tag pair (see section 4.12.1). Index entries may be formatted by placing a <UL> or <OL> tag after the head, before the first list item, and a

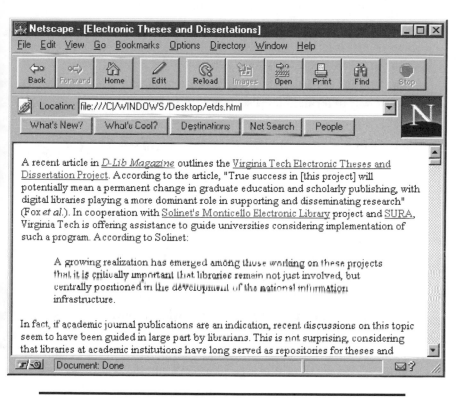

Figure 5.2 An Example of In-Text References in Hypertext

</UL> or </OL> tag after the last item and surrounding each item by the <P> . . . </P> tags (for an unbulleted list) or the <LI> . . . </LI> tags (for a bulleted list) as desired. If you have the necessary know-how and online resources, you might also consider installing a searchable index (an interactive feature that allows users to search a specific site for keywords or terms).

5.2.7 List of contributors

The list of contributors presents brief biographical information about the authors who contributed to a text. Italicize each author's name, or code it as an email link to the author's email address, if desired, using the <A HREF=" "> . . . </A> tag pair. Enclose each entry in the list within the <P> . . . </P> tag pair (see section 5.16). Creating two-way hypertextual links between bylines and the entries on the contributors can be an especially effective way to format these lists (see section 5.5).

PUBLISHING DOCUMENTS ON A COMPUTER NETWORK

5.3 File Organization

Locate all files relating to a particular document in the same directory, if possible, and, again if possible, include only files relating to the document in that directory. The cover page or opening page of the site, if applicable, should be named index.html if possible, so that it will be the default page for the site or directory. For example, http://chuma.cas.usf.edu/~walker/ will automatically open up the file at http://chuma.cas.usf.edu/~walker/index.html unless another file name is specified. All files may be saved in the default directory (~walker in this example) or in subdirectories created within the root directory. Links from the main page will allow readers easy access without long URLs.

5.4 Navigating and Frames

Since page numbers are irrelevant (or nonexistent) online, online authors must use a system that allows readers to navigate through their texts effectively. Shorter texts may use page anchors as navigation aids (see figure 5.3). Longer texts should separate large segments of text into separate computer files with unique URLs, and create navigational links between the URLs. Any segment of text much larger than two thousand words (or even less for WWW documents) should be formatted with a structure that permits effective navigation. Two common approaches to navigation are (1) to place hypertextual links either at the beginning of a file and/or at the end (see section 5.5) and (2) to use frames.

Authors should be aware that many readers will have difficulty using frames effectively unless they have access to frames-compatible browsers. Many sites that use frames thus offer a nonframes version as well. Nevertheless, frames can be an effective navigational aid if used carefully.

5.5 Links

Create hypertextual links when appropriate by surrounding the text you wish to serve as a link (or hot spot) with the tag pair <A HREF – " "> . . . </A>. This will create a link between the text and the referenced URL and will usually change the font color of the linked text to blue and underline it (in most browsers). Make sure that the text you choose to serve as a link is sufficiently explanatory of where the link will take the reader and as brief as possible (a page with too many long links can be difficult to read). Consider, too, that URLs outside your control may disappear over time; if necessary, you may want to include (as an appendix) a list of the external links used in your work, including a brief discussion of what was at the linked URL at the time. Each separate page of your own site should include a link back to either the cover

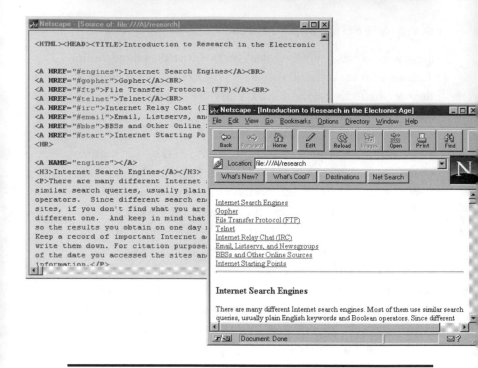

Figure 5.3 Using Page Anchors

page or the contents page and may also contain links to other parts of the document, if appropriate. An author should confirm that all links in a text are functioning properly (that is, a click on each highlighted term actually connects the reader to the appropriate reference site) before submitting or publishing an online text.

5.6 Colors

If you feel background colors or textures or font colors other than black are integral to your publication, you may use them but do so with extreme caution: they tend to be distracting and may decrease readability if overused. Reading onscreen is already more difficult than reading printed material, so anything that reduces the contrast between text and the background should be avoided. For this reason, it is best not to format text with color. If you are using colored fonts or backgrounds, however, you may also want to consider changing the default colors for linked text to avoid clashing. (See chapter 6 for a more detailed discussion of the pros and cons of color online.)

5.7 Spacing

Do not attempt to double-space text in online documents; this may be difficult to do and may cause more problems than it solves. Auto-wrap features enable text to fit within browser windows, regardless of what size window the user may select. Forcing extra spacing may defeat this and actually make the text harder to read onscreen. Even hard copy printouts may be adversely affected unless the hypertext author attempts to ensure that the text will fit on standard size paper (keeping in mind that U.S. and European paper standards differ), a task that can be most arduous given the many different printer programs, software defaults, and user changes.

5.8 Fonts

Use default fonts unless you must absolutely do otherwise; do not add color or a specific font face or size unless you must. Use only the header tag pairs—<H1> . . . </H1>, <H2> . . . </H2>, <H3> . . . </H3>, and so on—to indicate titles and subheads (see sections 4.15, 5.12, and 5.15). Allow body text to remain at default settings if possible. Readers often can override the fonts, font sizes, and font colors selected by an author, so any choices you make may not appear on the reader's screen.

5.9 Formatting Techniques

5.9.1 Boldface

See section 4.9.1. An author can format text in boldface online by enclosing it within the <B> . . . </B> tag pair. Use boldface sparingly and only when absolutely necessary. It should not be used to indicate emphasis.

5.9.2 Underlining and italics

Underlining is a formatting technique used online to designate a hypertextual link and should be reserved for this purpose in all but exceptional circumstances. There is no need to insert special codes to underline hypertext links for most WWW documents; the <A HREF=" ">... </A> tag pair will usually automatically format linked text. When absolutely necessary to underline certain text, however, enclose it within the <U>... </U> tag pair. Be aware, however, that many older browsers will not recognize these tags.

While italics are the preferred means to indicate emphasis, titles of large works (such as books, movies, etc.), foreign words, terminology, and other elements that are sometimes underlined in print texts, these elements should not be formatted identically online. Titles of large works should use the <CITE>... </CITE> tag pair; normal emphasis is accomplished with the <EM>... </EM> pair; and strong emphasis uses the <STRONG>... </STRONG> pair. HTML has a tag to include blinking text for added emphasis, but blinking text is inappropriate in academic writing. In all other cases, such as with foreign words, use the <I>... </I> tag pair to create italicized text. (See the discussion in section 4.9.2 for details.)

For ASCII text editors, email programs, and text-only browsers, such as Lynx, that do not recognize either italics or underlining, we recommend using the underscore character (_) before and after the text. For example:

The Columbia Guide to Online Style

Most of the other tags discussed above are also unreadable in text-only versions, so, to indicate emphasis in such formats, many users place asterisks (*) around the text they wish to emphasize. For example,

This text is emphasized

Asterisks are also sometimes used, especially in email messages, to indicate "emotes," or facial expressions, as in *grin*. Some ASCII authors may also surround text with emotes enclosed in angle brackets, thus allowing a mixture of face-to-face and print elements. For example: <SMILE>It's later than you think</SMILE>. And, of course, we have all seen :-), the sideways smiley face called an emoticon.

5.10 Special Characters

See section 4.10. To insert a special character in your text, you may use the appropriate ISO number set, preceded by "&#" and followed immediately by a semicolon. For example, "©" will appear as the copyright symbol © when viewed through a Web browser. You may also use the HTML character set for reserved characters (for example, "<" is the symbol for the left angle bracket, <).

5.11 Bylines

A byline indicates the author(s) of the work and other relevant information such as affiliation or geographic location. It should be placed at the very beginning of each document, on the title page if appropriate. Using the standard default font, list each author's first name followed by the middle initial and surname. On a separate line or lines include other relevant information such as date, and institutional affiliation. Use the line break tag, <BR>, or the <P> ... </P> tag pair (as appropriate) to separate items in the byline. Do not include a byline when submitting work for anonymous grading or review. (See also metatags in section 5.1.)

5.12 Titles

See section 4.12.

Titles of documents placed online also serve the important function of giving the document an identity to be referenced by those using search engines. Enclose the full title of a Web site or a larger online work within the <TITLE> ... </TITLE> tag pair in the head of each separate page that is part of the complete document, including any other relevant information (such as chapter number or title) as appropriate. This title may be repeated on each page by enclosing it within the <H1> ... </H1> tag pair in the body of the document. Chapter and section titles should then be enclosed within the <H2> ... </H2> tag pair, if applicable (see also sections 5.12.1 and 5.12.2 below).

5.12.1 Titles for Article- or Chapter-Length Projects

Place the article or chapter title immediately before the byline, enclosed within the <H2> ... </H2> tag pair (see section 4.12.1). Do not use all capital letters for titles, and it is not necessary to boldface, underline, or italicize them. For article- or chapter-length projects, the full title and the article or chapter title may be the same.

5.12.2 Titles for Book-Length Projects

In the case of book-length projects that consist of several online files, the title of the complete work should be included in the HTML head, enclosed within the <TITLE> ... </TITLE> tag pair, and repeated immediately before the byline, enclosed within the <H1> ... </H1> tag pair.

5.13 Section Numbers

Section numbers, which provide a constant and sequential system for referencing specific locations in a text, can be inserted in online texts if they will help readers locate information more easily. Hypertextual page anchors can serve similar purposes (see section 5.5). Section numbers may be manually inserted, or you may choose to format the sections using the <OL> . . . </OL> tag pair, enclosing each numbered section within the <LI> . . . </LI> tag pair.

5.14 Return Links

As a courtesy to your readers, include a return link and any other navigational links on every URL within your site. Return links are typically placed either at the bottom of a page or in a frame. If your document features a contents page, provide a link back to it. If your document does not have a linear organization, include a link back to your title page. A link taking readers back to the previous node, or page, is helpful in linear texts as well. Links to major divisions within a text are helpful but not essential.

5.15 Subheads

See section 4.15. For online subheads, use upper- and lowercase letters, not all capitals. Do not use boldface, italics, or underlining to format subheads unless it is absolutely necessary; instead, use the tag pairs listed in section 4.15.

5.16 Paragraphs

See section 4.16. To indicate paragraphs online, place a <P> tag at the beginning of each new paragraph and a </P> tag at the end of each paragraph. It is unnecessary to indent paragraphs in online documents.

5.17 Lists

5.17.1 Ordered Lists

See section 4.17.1, especially the discussion of how to format ordered lists in texts that will be submitted electronically for print publication. Ordered lists in online documents may also be "nested," that is, you may open multiple ordered lists within other lists to create an indented list similar in structure to an outline.

5.17.2 Unordered Lists

See section 4.17.2, especially the discussion of how to format unordered lists in both print and electronic form. As for ordered lists, unordered lists may be nested to create an indented listing.

5.18 Quotations

5.18.1 Block Quotations

See section 4.18.1, particularly the discussion of how to format block quotations in texts prepared electronically for submission for print publication. Do not change fonts for block quotations online.

5.18.2 Epigraphs

See section 4.18.2, particularly the discussion of how to format epigraphs in texts submitted in electronic form for print publication. An epigraph will be distinguishable from a block quotation by its positioning at the very front of a text and by the inclusion of the author's name and the source title.

5.19 Note References

See section 4.19. Note numbers in online documents can be placed in superscript by using the ^{. . .} tag pair. However, a more dynamic approach would be to create a hypertextual link between body text and notes placed elsewhere in the document. See sections 5.2.3 and 5.5.

5.20 Artwork

See section 4.20. Artwork for online publications will almost always be stored in computer files separate from the body text, with

each piece located within the text by means of the <IMG SRC=
" "> tag, which places artwork stored at a separate URL as a
graphic file on the page at the indicated location. You may define
the parameters of the image file within the <IMG SRC> tag by including other HTML codes, such as "ALT=" (which assigns a description name to graphic files for readers without graphical
browsers) or the "HEIGHT" and "WIDTH" commands (which allow the author to specify the number of pixels the graphic image
will encompass). For example, <IMG SRC="http://www.usf.
edu/graphics/usfcol.gif" ALT="The University of South Florida"
HEIGHT=160 WIDTH=220> is the tag used to place the logo at
the top of the home page for the University of South Florida at
http://www.usf.edu/.

Authors must make sure that graphics files are scaled to use as
little computer memory as possible. Avoid images larger than 25K
(10K and below is preferable), and do not allow a single URL to
include more than 200K of artwork. Authors may align artwork
flush left, center, or flush right; but flush left is the default. GIF
and JPEG file formats are currently the standard for artwork published online.

5.20.1 Tables

See section 4.20.1. Most tables can be effectively composed online
using the table functions supported by HTML. Avoid using unnecessary formatting features—i.e., centering or justifying text,
changing fonts, and using boldface, italics, or underlining—unless absolutely necessary. More complex tables, however, require
special attention. These may be produced in print, digitized using
a scanner, and inserted as GIF or JPEG files when necessary. Use
tables with caution, however, because text-only browsers such as
Lynx do not recognize table codes and can make information contained within <TABLE> . . . </TABLE> tag pairs very difficult to
read.

5.20.2 Illustrations

See section 4.20.2.

5.20.3 Figures

See section 4.20.3.

5.20.4 Graphics

See section 4.20.4. In addition to adding graphics in GIF or JPEG formats, authors of online documents can create simple horizontal lines to enhance readability by using the <HR> tag. The length and width of the <HR> tag can also be defined by inserting the appropriate codes within the angle brackets (for instance, <HR SIZE=2 WIDTH=500 ALIGN=Center> will create a horizontal rule centered on a page extending 500 pixels across the page and 2 pixels thick. Icons, buttons, image maps (graphics with certain areas defined as links to discrete URLs), and other graphics used for navigational purposes online may be helpful when used appropriately; however, keep graphics simple and functional. Animated bullets and blinking text are unnecessary for most academic documents and can be extremely distracting to readers.

5.20.5 Photographs

See section 4.20.5. Photographs must first be digitized (scanned) in order to be displayed online. Reducing photographs from 256 or more colors to 16 colors when digitizing is a particularly effective means of reducing file sizes for most online applications. Cropping pictures to exclude extraneous backgrounds can also be helpful. Sizing graphics (preferably using a program designed to work with scanned photographic images) to fit the desired space on the Web page (using the "HEIGHT" and "WIDTH" commands in the <IMG SRC> tag) can also reduce image sizes; however, these tags will not reduce the file size and can cause considerable distortions of some images.

5.21 Diskettes

See "Preparing Diskettes" (page 148) in the previous chapter.

5.21.1 Naming Computer Files

See section 4.21. Note that files submitted to an editor or publisher of online documents exchanged through a network may use larger file names and extensions (for instance, "englishpages.html" is an acceptable file name online but not for most DOS and Windows 3.x applications). Names of files to be exchanged on diskette, however, should have file names of no more than eight characters and file extensions of no more than three characters to allow for portability across platforms.

5.21.2 Sending Diskettes Through the Mail

See section 4.22.

6

Beyond Basic Style
Additional Considerations
for Online Authors

The purpose of *The Columbia Guide* is to establish the rudimentary building blocks of online style so that the widest possible range of academic authors and readers can use electronic resources more reliably and thus more effectively. These guidelines are not intended to prevent authors from experimenting with emerging forms. In this chapter we discuss some important issues for more advanced authoring, including fundamental considerations such as file formats, Internet protocols, and copyright, as well as more intricate concerns such as browser compatibility and document design for online readers with impaired vision.

Effective design principles for more advanced online documents are, at present, very elusive. The dream is for standards such as SGML and XML (which, as of the late 1990s, is on the horizon) to allow authors to mark up documents with logical, generic tags so that, as publication technologies continue to develop, the same texts can be enhanced by the new production techniques without requiring substantial revision. Until this dream is realized, authors must continue to struggle to balance functionality and design.

A detailed examination of advanced hypertextual and multimedia design principles is beyond the scope of this book. The best attempt we have seen so far is the *Yale Center for Advanced Instructional Media Web Style Guide*, authored by Patrick J. Lynch and Sarah Horton, at http://info.med.yale.edu/caim/manual/index.html.

The Columbia Guide, in embracing the universality of HTML/ SGML logic, emphasizes stability and accessibility over graphic design. Guides to elaborate online design, such as the Yale guide, favor graphic design at the expense of universality. Ideally, authors in the future will not have to choose between accessibility and robust design as they do now. Readers should consult online updates of *The Columbia Guide* at http://www.columbia.edu/cu/cup/cgos for the latest information on the continuing struggle to establish new standards for advanced document design.

Formats and Protocols

Different word-processing applications and platforms already complicate the task of formulating standardized instructions for producing documents to be printed out, and further complications ensue when one attempts to establish standardized guidelines for preparing electronic versions of these manuscripts for submission for print publication. Of course, print publication is not likely to cease in the foreseeable future, but the time and costs it entails, coupled with increases in the ease of use and accessibility of powerful electronic information services, demand that authors and publishers begin to familiarize themselves thoroughly with electronic protocols as more and more authors, publishers, and users of information turn to online venues. To this end, then, some standards must be formulated to ease the transition.

When exchanging electronic copies of files created using word processors, it is necessary to ensure that the software programs required to read these files are available to the recipient; i.e., if you create a file using *Word for MacIntosh,* you (or someone else) may need to translate it into a format that can be read using *Word* or *WordPerfect* for the PC. ASCII text formats will eliminate all the formatting codes but will be readable in text-only form across most platforms. Rich-text formats (i.e., RTF) allow some formatting codes (such as italics, boldface, and underlining) to be retained but may lose other important features (such as tables or columns); in addition, they may sometimes be difficult to translate across platforms. For now, therefore, we recommend saving most word-processed files in *WordPerfect 5.1* format (regardless of the program you use to create it or read it) as this seems to translate the most readily, retaining important formatting as well as text. For electronic publications, many newer word processors and HTML editors can automatically convert files to SGML, HTML, or ASCII formats as required. However, many of these conversions are clunky, adding unnecessary tags or overlooking important elements. Thus, for the present, authors and publishers need to be familiar with the necessary commands to format documents for specific types of publication. As standards develop, however, it is likely that programs to translate files automatically between formats will become more automated and, with luck, more reliable.

Probably the most well-known online application is electronic mail, or email, which allows users to communicate asynchronously, that is, to send messages to each other to be read later. Newer email clients allow users to include non-ASCII formatting (such as different fonts and colors) as well as graphics and even audio files in the body of an email message, although to read these elements, the recipient must have access to a similar email client program. Both newer email clients and older text-only ones, however, allow users to attach various files, thereby retaining all the formats and codes used in their preparation. For example, a file produced using *WordPerfect 8.0* contains various formatting codes that can only be read using a software program designed to support these codes. If a user attaches such files to an email message, however, they will be transmitted with all these codes intact, the same as if they were shipped on diskette but in far less time. The files may then be downloaded to a personal computer and read using the correct software application. Authors and publishers are already finding this a quicker, cheaper, and more convenient way to transmit files intended for print as well as electronic publication.

File Transfer Protocol (FTP) is a means of moving electronic files from one location to another on a network. Using FTP, the user may transfer files from a personal computer (the "local host") to a network server (the "remote host") to send as attached files via email or to store on an FTP site where other users may access and download them (also using an FTP client) to their own computer. FTP clients (software programs that handle the transfer) are available in both text-only and graphical versions, and most FTP sites can be accessed using a Web client program called a "browser" and the ftp://address format. One of the most useful applications available, FTP seems also to be one of the most confusing for novices. Moreover, with the increasing popularity of the WWW, many documents that once resided at FTP sites are being converted to HTML formats. For larger files, however, many sites offer the option of accessing the file online in a Web browser or downloading it from an FTP site. Newer point-and-click FTP clients and faster connection speeds make for quicker and easier transmission of files, and the ability of WWW browsers to access ftp:// addresses is making file transfers increasingly more seamless and transparent. This trend is likely to continue as more people use online services to transfer information and files.

Gopher, a menu-driven system for locating and organizing information on the Internet, was one of the earliest attempts to make navigation of the morass of information online quicker, easier, and more efficient. However, gopher protocols are quickly being replaced by newer technologies, especially HTML protocols. Information at gopher sites can be accessed using either a gopher client (usually in a text-only format) or a Web browser and the gopher://address format. Although gopher offers its own search protocols (such as Archie, Veronica, and Jughead), most WWW search engines can also search gopherspace. But with the increasing popularity of graphical WWW browsers and search engines, it is likely that more and more gopher sites will migrate to these protocols in the future, and gopher protocols may ultimately become obsolete.

Files in both FTP and gopher sites may be in any one of a number of formats. Often available are text versions (i.e., ASCII) that can be read using any text editor or word processor; files created using specific word-processing codes or in Print Document Format (PDF) may require specific programs or applications to be readable. Many files are also compressed, using one of a number of different file compression methods available (such as .zip, .lhc, or .tar); these may require the user to have access to specific uncompression programs. Usually, the file extension will tell the knowledgeable user what type of application may be necessary to read or use the file after it is downloaded. Again, it is probable that some standardization of formats will develop to allow greater accessibility across programs and platforms. Many Web browsers will already automatically find the necessary programs to read files and offer users the option of downloading them, if necessary. More than likely, this process, too, will become increasingly transparent, allowing greater accessibility across programs and platforms.

Telnet protocols allow users to log on to a remote computer and execute commands or access files that reside on it. Many PPP (Point-to-Point Protocol) accounts use a telnet client program in order to access the shell, or operating system, on the remote host. Telnet protocols are also used to access MOOs and MUDs and many library databases. Most browsers, if properly configured, can access telnet sites by using the telnet:// form of the URL to open the configured telnet client automatically. However, some commercial information providers, such as *America Online,* offer the use of telnet protocols only if the user downloads and installs a separate compatible telnet client, while many online service providers do not provide ready access to telnet protocols at all. With the development of technology that allows for real-time communication between local and remote hosts using graphical interfaces (i.e., through browsers), it is likely that the use of current telnet applications may become more and more restricted to use by those administering the online services.

Although many people still connect to online services using text-only communication protocols, faster processors, faster communications hardware (i.e., faster modems and digital technologies), and decreasing costs have prompted a move to the use of graphical interfaces for accessing the Internet, usually via PPP. This, in turn, is prompting changes in how information is made available online. Hypertext Transfer Protocol (or HTTP) is a means of transferring information online between remote computers that permits the inclusion of hypertext links (i.e, designated "hot spots" to which the user can point in order to be connected automatically to other sites), as well as multimedia elements such as colors, fonts, graphics, audio, and video. In order to access information using HTTP, the user must have some kind of browser. Older, text-only browsers such as Lynx are still available, and, in some instances, quicker, because they do not support the time-consuming transfer of large and often unwieldy graphics files; the user of such a browser may need to download multimedia files included in the text for viewing using other programs. GUI (or graphical-user-interface) browsers, such as *Netscape* and *Microsoft Internet Explorer,* have gained in popularity, however, and many HTTP files created for these browsers may be difficult (or even impossible) to read in text-only formats because they include codes and/or formatting, such as tables or special fonts, not recognized by older browsers. Probably these formats, too, will soon become more standardized—making it easier for users to access information online without the necessity of installing specific browsers or software applications—as demand for compatibility continues to escalate.

Information is currently available electronically from a variety of sources: on CD-ROMs, from BBSs and information providers such as *America Online* or *Microsoft Network,* as well as on the Internet. Some libraries and universities subscribe to electronic information services such as *FirstSearch* and are replacing CD-ROM and print-only versions of their materials with World Wide Web access; some of these services already make full texts available to subscribers online. Other sources of academic materials, such as University Microforms International (UMI)—which now offers copies of theses and dissertations in print or microform that can be searched for and ordered on the WWW—may soon make files available to researchers electronically via email or on the WWW as universities begin allowing (or even requiring) scholars to submit work in electronic formats. The library of the future will most likely rely more and more on the digital preservation of materials, electronic catalogs, and electronic distribution methods. But these changes may entail more than merely translating print features into their electronic counterparts. Changes in the technologies of reading, writing, research, and publishing may also prompt changes in our very conception of the text itself. The ease of self-publication, too, means that more information will be available, information that may need to be evaluated and perhaps cataloged as part of the scholarly conversation.

Accessibility and Stability

Documents in cyberspace may move or disappear without notice. Even documents that have not moved or disappeared entirely may change so that previous "editions" no longer exist. However, simply because we cannot yet guarantee that works will remain static or permanent does not mean we can disallow their importance to the conversation at the moment when they do exist, and indeed some standards for ensuring the accessibility and stability of electronic resources have already developed. Just as rare books and out-of-print works may sometimes be uncovered with a little detective work, so, too, can online works sometimes be relocated. Search engines can often find files that have moved, and contacting the author or the system administrator for the domain server (the site where the information was previously published online) may help to track down documents that have disappeared. These standards will continue to change and develop as technology itself changes and develops and as electronic writing, reading, and publishing become more and more the norm rather than the exception.

Persistent Uniform Resource Locators (PURLs) and Uniform Resource Names (URNs)

Since URLs can change with alarming frequency, the Online Computer Library Center (OCLC) has developed a system known as PURLs (Persistent Uniform Resource Locators) that supports the maintenance of stable Internet addresses. When you point to a PURL, it will automatically connect to the actual URL of a document, even if the document has moved—provided that the PURL has been maintained. Uniform Resource Names (URNs) represent another attempt to provide some stability of online sources. URNs, as proposed at a meeting hosted by Keith Moore at the University of Tennessee, assign a unique name to online files, regardless of their location, making them easier to search for on the WWW. And although neither standard guarantees that a document will remain available, both seek to ensure some stability.

Archives

Many people and organizations are attempting to find ways to archive online documents reliably, although the mass of information published online daily makes this a rather prohibitive venture. Great strides have already been made, however: Libraries are looking at ways to archive information and make online scholarship even more accessible by making works easier to catalog and thus easier to search. Many online journals, listservs, and other sites have also created archives, some of which are searchable. Again, some standardization could help to make this project more feasible.

Copyright Considerations

A 1995 report by the Information Infrastructure Task Force recommended that the U.S. Copyright Office require copies of online documents on paper or, alternatively, on diskette or some other more permanent electronic medium to be filed with them. The Copyright Office has required the deposit of published print works only in recent times; further requiring deposit of copies of work published online may be ineffectual as such copies may not accurately represent the work as it appears online. Differing attitudes of other countries toward copyright further complicate the issue of protecting the rights of authors and publishers online.

Recommendations to authors to save copies of files or documents that they cite or include as external links in their works may sometimes be construed as violation of copyright under current laws, and the international content of the Internet makes it difficult to know exactly which laws apply. When it is necessary to print out or save copies of electronic works, it might be advisable to attempt to contact the author for permission if in doubt. If this is not feasible, retain as much of the copyright information and documentation of the source as possible so that an attempt can be made to locate the author should the need arise. Until legislators (and diplomats) standardize guidelines, it is important that we at least consider the ethical implications of our use of online information and sources.

Considerations for Advanced Design

Electronic versions of scholarly documents may include elements not found in traditional works. Many word processors now allow for embedding applications such as spreadsheet software or links that automatically open WWW browsers and connect to online addresses (many newer word processors automatically reformat URLs and other Internet addresses included in the text, usually changing the color and/or font size, underlining the address, and automatically creating a hypertext link). Some of these applications (usually read-only versions) are then saved along with the document text, graphics, and other parts of the file. WWW documents may also include animated graphics, audio, and video files (and the software necessary to read them). The speed of technological development is likely to continue to escalate in the foreseeable future, and authors must consider the impact this has on their work.

Browsers and Plug-Ins

Software applications come and go, and new applications are released daily, many available for free downloading online. Providing a link to the download site or embedding necessary software applications within a file are ways of ensuring their availability to the reader. Scholarship that relies on specific platforms and software may be inaccessible to many, however, and should be used with caution. Moving to a platform-independent environment may eventually help to alleviate this problem.

External Links

Links to external sites can also cause problems, as sites mutate, move, or disappear entirely. One possible solution, used by the online journal *Kairos: A Journal for Teachers of Writing in Webbed Environments* (http://english.ttu.edu/kairos/), requires authors to submit a list of all external links, annotating the links so that, in the event one no longer works, the reader will at least have access to a summary of what the author intended to point to. The following is an example of such an annotated list.

(Please note: all links were operational as of March 3, 1997)

- The link *Argos* originally pointed to http://argos.evansville.edu/
about.htm, a specialized search engine that promises to return only
hits that have been deemed "valuable" as scholarship by a team of
peer reviewers.

- The link *Agrippa: A Book of the Dead* originally pointed to
http://www.astro.utoronto.ca/~reid/htmldocs/agrippa.html, the text
of a "book" by William Gibson and artist Dennis Ashbaugh that, although disguised as a mild-mannered traditional text, ceases to exist
upon being read. This book, then, is an example of the ephemerality
of all text, both traditional print and hypertext.

Other suggestions require authors to save electronic copies of
external links. This would not only require obtaining permissions
but could be impracticable, as linked sites may contain links to
other external sites, ad infinitum. Pointing only to those sites that
are relatively stable and reliable is both limiting and risky, although some programs now notify an interested user when a site
changes. Further development of such programs is one solution
for the future. It is equally feasible that the Web will develop to a
point where incoming links will be automatically recognized and
linked pages will automatically be updated to direct users to the
correct location. At any rate, omitting external links to make each
work a stand-alone file would only eliminate some of the value of
publishing on the World Wide Web.

File Size

File sizes, as explained in more detail in chapter 5, should usually
be kept as small as possible. Bandwidth, connection speeds, and
storage capabilities are still limited, and files that are difficult or
time consuming to download or browse may tax a reader's pa-
tience and resources. What makes most files large and unwieldy
are graphics and multimedia elements, not the text itself. Files

destined for print can usually ignore byte size because, for them, the ultimate number of pages of printed matter is what counts. However, for electronic files, the number of bytes determines the time and space a given file will require to access and store.

Backgrounds, Colors, Fonts, and Graphics

Readers now expect documents to make at least some use of specialized backgrounds, colors, fonts, graphics, and multimedia elements. Advances in word processing and desktop publishing capabilities for most users have allowed authors to incorporate these elements readily into their printed texts, and a WWW document consisting only of plain blocks of black text on a white or gray background may be disconcerting online. Any graphics and colors used should enhance the readability and visual attractiveness of a document, but they should also serve a purpose. Colors convey messages—certain colors are soothing, others are energizing; they can also add to (or detract from) the overall readability of a page. To be safe, as noted in chapter 5, use backgrounds, colors, fonts, graphics, and multimedia elements sparingly and with caution. Text documents may lose important typographical elements when saved in ASCII (text) formats or converted to other software formats. Many point-and-click email editors allow the author to embed links, use fonts and colors, and include graphics and other hypertextual features in their electronic mail messages. These features, however, may depend on the reader using the same, or a similar, email client to read the messages. Readers using a text-only mail program, such as Pine, will see only a plain text version of the message, from which all the author's intended emphasis, links, colors, and other elements have been stripped. Graphics are translated into attached files, requiring the user to download them for viewing in a separate program. Even if all the personalizing features are downloaded, users have the option of overriding any text and background colors that an author selects, so the intended effects may never even be seen by the reader. An extreme example involves the use of black backgrounds with white text, a practice popular in WWW documents, especially with students. What many do not realize is that, to those familiar with the online world, the black background makes a political statement about cyber censorship (many netizens, or citizens of the Net, changed Web page backgrounds to black to protest proposed censorship legislation). In addition, this combination of background and text color is to some extent a hindrance to easy translation to print: if a reader hits the print button to translate the file or document into print as it is, he or she will be left holding only a blank page. Backgrounds may not print, so what the reader gets is white text on white paper—in other words, nothing at all.

Browser-Dependent Sites

Different versions of browsers, and different browsers, can cause problems for authors as well as readers. Elements of hypertext or hypermedia documents, such as frames, image maps, animated graphics, audio and video files—even some fonts and colors— may not be visible or may appear differently on different browsers. Many sites on the WWW display the message "Best viewed with . . ." and may include a link to the download site for a particular browser. Some browsers and software, however, may require specific platforms or processing speeds, or fees or other factors can prevent their ready accessibility. While we can probably expect some standardization of browser capabilities to emerge in the not-too-distant future, for now authors and online publishers should carefully consider whether or not to use specific applications within their online documents. One alternative is to make available text-only versions of documents and files, which require minimal resources. See also the suggestions below for making WWW documents user-friendly for the visually impaired.

Conventions for the Visually Impaired

In addition to considerations of platforms, software, and browser capabilities, authors need to do whatever they can to make sure that their work is accessible to those who are visually handicapped. Even though the WWW is primarily a visual medium, there are ways to make online documents and files as user friendly as possible even for the visually impaired. Braille keyboards and printers, voice recognition software, and software that can recognize and read files to the user are, of course, possibilities, and some of these solutions are already in use. A few simple considerations, however, can greatly aid those with reduced vision without adding too much complexity. For example, whenever possible, WWW authors should consider offering text-only versions of their work. The link to the text version should be placed near the beginning of the page. Use high contrast between text and background (e.g., white backgrounds and black text and/or larger fonts). Avoid tables and frames, or include links to text versions of each table and nonframe versions of files. In addition, include descriptions of images and image-map links in text versions. The same consideration may be shown to others, such as the hearing impaired, by including written descriptions of sound files. Many of the suggestions offered for making texts more accessible to the visually or hearing impaired also make sense for text-only browsers, such as Lynx, because, as noted above, not all elements allowed in graphical browsers readily transfer to different formats.

Conclusion

In the future, we can perhaps expect more standardization of platforms and browsers, more translatability among various software packages, and more stability as libraries do what they do best: find reliable means to catalog information and provide access to it. We can also most likely expect that the mass of information online will continue to proliferate and morph into new forms.

Access is likely to be less of a problem, as more people acquire faster and more powerful machines with faster connections capable of accessing large multimedia applications and databases, and as increased bandwidth becomes readily available. From the days when books were lovingly and meticulously hand-copied by monks and thus prohibitively expensive for the masses (and so large and unwieldy that a reader had to stand at a podium) to modern times when printing presses and changes in economic and educational structures have made low-cost books readily available, we have seen literacy and its forms and expressions change in many ways. Likewise, we can expect more changes, greater accessibility, lower costs, and, conceivably, a wider variety of interests represented in published works online as economic and other barriers to publication are removed. Of course, this means that the gatekeeper functions—the masses of editors, publishers, reviewers, and library purchasers who guaranteed, at least somewhat, the reliability of our sources (or at least their marketability)—must now become the responsibility of individual readers, as they determine the value (and validity) of works for themselves.

Changes are taking place so quickly, it is difficult to keep up. And for a print publication, such as this book, even to attempt to set forth standards is quite ambitious. But the guidelines set forth here do more than merely capture a given moment in time—bottling the ether. This examination of the various elements of academic works and their translation—when they can be translated—into standardized formats may make us better able to consider new elements as they emerge and reconsider existing ones in the future. This book should not, like so many current attempts, be obsolete even before its publication. Instead, it should continue to be useful at least until the next edition and perhaps even until print technology is itself obsolete.

WORKS CITED

Information Infrastructure Task Force. "Intellectual Property and the National Information Infrastructure: The Report of the Working Group on Intellectual Property Rights." Sept. 1995. http://www.uspto.gov:80/web/offices/com/doc/ipnii/ipnii.txt (15 Jan. 1998).

Kairos: A Journal for Teachers of Writing in Webbed Environments. http://english.ttu.edu/kairos/ (25 May 1998).

Lynch, Patrick J., and Sarah Horton. "Yale Center for Advanced Instructional Media Web Style Guide." 1997. http://info.med.yale.edu/caim/manual/index.html (25 May 1998).

ISO Latin-1 Characters and Control Characters

Character	Decimal	Entity Reference	Character	Decimal	Entity Reference
NUL	0		SOH	1	
STX	2		ETX	3	
EOT	4		ENQ	5	
ACK	6		BEL	7	
BS	8		HT	9	
LF	10		VT	11	
NP	12		CR	13	
SO	14		SI	15	
DLE	16		DC1	17	
DC2	18		DC3	19	
DC4	20		NAK	21	
SYN	22		ETB	23	
CAN	24		EM	25	
SUB	26		ESC	27	
FS	28		GS	29	
RS	30		US	31	
SP	32		!	33	
"	34	"	#	35	
$	36		%	37	
&	38	&	'	39	
(	40		)	41	
*	42		+	43	
,	44		-	45	
.	46		/	47	
0	48		1	49	
2	50		3	51	
4	52		5	53	
6	54		7	55	
8	56		9	57	
:	58		;	59	
<	60	<	=	61	
>	62	>	?	63	
@	64		A	65	
B	66		C	67	
D	68		E	69	
F	70		G	71	
H	72		I	73	
J	74		K	75	
L	76		M	77	
N	78		O	79	
P	80		Q	81	

Character	Decimal	Entity Reference	Character	Decimal	Entity Reference
R	82		S	83	
T	84		U	85	
V	86		W	87	
X	88		Y	89	
Z	90		[	91	
\	92		]	93	
^	94		_	95	
`	96		a	97	
b	98		c	99	
d	100		e	101	
f	102		g	103	
h	104		i	105	
j	106		k	107	
l	108		m	109	
n	110		o	111	
p	112		q	113	
r	114		s	115	
t	116		u	117	
v	118		w	119	
x	120		y	121	
z	122		{	123	
|	124		}	125	
~	126		DEL	127	
	160		¡	161	&iexcl;
¢	162	&cent;	£	163	&pound;
¤	164	&curren;	¥	165	&yen;
¦	166	&brvbar;	§	167	&sect;
¨	168	&uml;	©	169	&copy;
ª	170	&ordf;	«	171	&laqno;
¬	172	&not;	—	173	&shy;
®	174	&reg;	–	175	&hibar;
°	176	&deg;	±	177	&plusmn;
²	178	&sup2;	³	179	&sup3;
´	180	&acute;	µ	181	&micro;
¶	182	&para;	·	183	&middot;
¸	184	&cedil;	¹	185	&sup1;
º	186	&ordm;	»	187	&raquo;
¼	188	&frac14;	½	189	&frac12;
¾	190	&frac34;	¿	191	&iquest;
À	192	&Agrave;	Á	193	&Aacute;
Â	194	&Acirc;	Ã	195	&Atilde;
Ä	196	&Auml;	Å	197	&Aring;

Character	Decimal	Entity Reference	Character	Decimal	Entity Reference
Æ	198	Æ	Ç	199	Ç
È	200	È	É	201	É
Ê	202	Ê	Ë	203	Ë
Ì	204	Ì	Í	205	Í
Î	206	Î	Ï	207	Ï
Ð	208	Ð	Ñ	209	&Ntidle;
Ò	210	Ò	Ó	211	Ó
Ô	212	Ô	Õ	213	Õ
Ö	214	Ö	×	215	×
Ø	216	Ø	Ù	217	Ù
Ú	218	Ú	Û	219	Û
Ü	220	Ü	Ý	221	Ý
Þ	222	Þ	ß	223	ß
à	224	à	á	225	á
â	226	â	ã	227	ã
ä	228	ä	å	229	å
æ	230	æ	ç	231	ç
è	232	è	é	233	é
ê	234	ê	ë	235	ë
ì	236	ì	í	237	í
î	238	î	ï	239	ï
ð	240	ð	ñ	241	ñ
ò	242	ò	ó	243	ó
ô	244	ô	õ	245	õ
ö	246	ö	÷	247	÷
ø	248	ø	ù	249	ù
ú	250	ú	û	251	û
ü	252	ü	ý	253	ý
þ	254	þ	ÿ	255	ÿ

GLOSSARY

address The location of a specific site or document, usually including the domain name and the path to access a particular file.

alias Many Internet sites and electronic mail configurations allow the user to designate an alias or fictitious name. Many electronic mail programs also use a login name rather than the user's actual name. Programs such as MOOs and MUDs and Internet Relay Chat (IRC) usually allow the user to select a character name to use. When an author's name is not available, the alias may be used instead.

American Standard Code for Information Interchange *See* ASCII.

anchor A hypertext tag used to create a link. In addition to linking to external documents or files, anchors can link to specific sections within the same document or file by specifying anchor names within a document.

applet A program written in Java scripting language that can be included in an HTML file by using the <APPLET CODE> , </APPLET> tags to call up the program from a discrete location. *See also* Java.

angle brackets Symbols (< >) used in Hypertext Markup Language to designate hypertext commands. They should not be used around URLs or email addresses as they may cause confusion with software applications and add unnecessary complexity.

archive A location where files or collections of files are stored for later access. Many WWW archives are searchable and use various download and compression protocols, depending on the site and the types of files stored.

ASCII American Standard Code for Information Interchange. A seven-bit code representing 128 characters that is capable of translating letters, numbers, and special characters across a wide variety of platforms. *See also* ISO Latin-1.

asynchronous Used to designate communication or commands that are not simultaneous. In Internet communication, asynchronous communication refers to electronic mail and other communications wherein messages are not dependent on timing. *See also* synchronous.

BBS Bulletin Board Service. A service that provides dial-in access to remote users, enabling them to access files and information and to communicate with other users. Files reside on the host computer and can be shared and downloaded by authorized users. Most BBSs require the user to obtain an account on the service, either for free or for a fee. BBSs may be very small, consisting of only a dozen or so users, or extremely large, with millions of subscribers. Many BBSs offer subscribers varying levels of Internet access as well.

Boolean operators Used by many Internet and library searches, these are operators such as "AND," "OR," "NOT," or "NEAR" that limit or define search terms in a query. For example, "movies OR films" returns a list of all documents or WWW pages found that contain either term; "films NOT movies" returns a list of only those sites that do not include the word "movies."

browser A software program that allows users to access the World Wide Web and move through hypertextual links. Some browsers, such as Lynx, offer text-only versions, while browsers such as *Netscape* and *Microsoft Internet Explorer* offer graphical interfaces and use point-and-click technology.

Bulletin Board Service *See* BBS.

CD-ROM Compact Disc, Read-Only Memory. An electronic storage medium designed to hold large amounts of information.

CGI Common Gateway Interface. A scripting language that allows hypertext documents to be customized and documents produced, usually in real time, in response to user input.

chat A term used to refer to any one of several synchronous, real-time communication programs that allow multiple users to connect and communicate with each other, usually by inputting text or commands on a keyboard. *See also* IRC.

clickable images *See* image maps.

client A client is a software program installed on the host computer or on the user's personal computer that facilitates certain protocols. Client programs are available for various platforms for FTP, gopher, telnet, email, synchronous communications, and a wide array of other common online uses.

command-line interface A computer interface that requires users to input commands at a prompt. For example, in DOS users enter the command "dir" at a C:\ prompt in order to see a listing, or directory, of files.

Common Gateway Interface *See* CGI.

Compact Disc, Read-Only Memory *See* CD-ROM.

cyberspace A term coined by William Gibson in his cyberpunk novel *Neuromancer* to refer to the entire online world, the computerized space in which programs and files reside and communication takes place.

database A collection of files, usually containing common fields or data records, that allows data to be organized, searched, and manipulated for use in various ways.

directory A structure for organizing files on a computer or host, similar to a file folder containing individual documents.

Disk Operating System *See* DOS.

DNS Domain Name Server. This refers to the host machine or computer that provides storage and access to files for a particular domain name.

domain name The unique alias for a specific IP (*which see*) address that is used to connect to an individual site or page on the Internet.

Domain Name Server *See* DNS.

DOS Disk Operating System. Software that controls the computer's operation. Other operating systems include Windows95, MacIntosh, and Unix.

email Electronic mail. A system that allows users to send messages on the Internet or through other electronic systems using modems and telephone lines or some other kind of cabling connection. On most systems, messages are received almost instantaneously and can be read and replied to entirely online.

ethernet A means of connecting computers in a network that uses cables for communication. Because they provide direct access, ethernet connections to an ISP (*which see*) are much faster than dial-in services.

eXtensible Markup Language. *See* XML.

file A single electronic program, document, image, or element with a discrete name.

file compression A method of reducing file sizes by encoding their contents. Compressing files allows for faster transmission times.

File Transfer Protocol *See* FTP.

frame On World Wide Web sites, frames are designated HTML elements that permit certain information to be retained onscreen in the browser window while other WWW pages are accessed within the frame's borders.

FTP File Transfer Protocol. A means of moving files between remote machines.

GIF Graphics Interchange Format. A commercial graphics format widely used for images on the WWW. *See also* JPEG, MPEG.

Gopher A menu-driven system for organizing and accessing files and programs on the Internet.

Graphics Interchange Format *See* GIF.

hard copy A paper printout of a file or document stored electronically.

hard page break A manual word-processing command that forces a page break. Pressing the *Ctrl* and *Enter* keys simultaneously creates a hard page break in most word-processing applications.

hard return A manual word-processing command that ends one line of text and begins a new one, typically used to end one paragraph and begin a new one. A single hard return is created by pressing the *Enter* key once. *See also* soft return.

hardware Physical computer equipment and peripherals, as opposed to the programs or instructions that run on the computer. *See also* software.

host A computer that allows one or more users on a network to share resources and files.

HTML Hypertext Markup Language. A language used to create World Wide Web documents that allows the author to include links and other features such as graphics that may be read using Hypertext Transfer Protocol. *See also* HTTP, hypertext.

HTTP Hypertext Transfer Protocol. The process by which hypertext files (WWW pages) are transferred between computers on the Internet.

hypermedia Hypertext documents or files that contain multimedia elements, such as graphics, audio, or video files, as well as text.

hypertext A term used to designate text in electronic files formatted as a link to other information. Also used to refer to documents published electronically that include hypertextual links.

Hypertext Markup Language *See* HTML.

Hypertext Transfer Protocol *See* HTTP.

image maps Also sometimes called "imaps" or "clickable images," these are graphic images with specific areas of the image mapped out or designated as links to other sites or other sections within the same file or WWW page.

imaps *See* image maps.

Internet An international network of computers originally designed by the U.S. Department of Defense to ensure communication abilities in the event of a catastrophe. The Internet today connects millions of individual users, universities, governments, businesses, and organizations, using telephone lines, fiber-optic cabling, ethernet connections, and other means. The Internet is different from an internet (small *i*), which is any interconnected network of computers.

Internet Service Provider *See* ISP.

intranet An interconnected network of computers, usually within a single organization, similar to a LAN or WAN. Intranets allow users to share files and communicate with each other using browsers, email, and other applications designed for Internet communication. Intranets may allow access to the Internet; however, they cannot be accessed from outside and thus provide a measure of security for their users.

IP Internet Protocol. The method used to route packets of information using the best available route. The Internet was designed as a means of ensuring communication in the event of a catastrophe. Thus should one route become unavailable or disabled, IP addressing will immediately reroute the information.

IRC Internet Relay Chat. A real-time synchronous communication site on the Internet that allows multiple users to log in at the same time, connect to various "rooms" (or channels, sometimes called "chat rooms") organized around topics of mutual interest, and "talk" to each other, usually by inputting text on a keyboard. Multimedia computers can also use types of software, such as Internet Phone, that use IRC channels to allow voice communication rather than keyboard input.

ISO International Standards Organization. An international organization in Geneva, Switzerland, dedicated to developing standards for the open exchange of information across different terminals, computers, networks, and applications.

ISO Latin-1 An eight-bit character set, similar to ASCII, that allows 256 characters instead of the 128 characters allowed by the seven-bit code. *See also* ASCII.

ISP Internet Service Provider. A service that allows users to connect to the Internet, often by dial-in connections.

Java A scripting language that allows users to include programs, called "applets" (*which see*), that can be transferred along with other elements in a hypertextual file to Java-enabled browsers, that is, browsers that recognize the Java scripting language.

Joint Photographic Experts Group *See* JPEG.

JPEG Joint Photographic Experts Group. A standard for photographic-quality image compression on the WWW. *See also* GIF, MPEG.

LAN Local Area Network. Two or more computers linked together and sharing resources allocated by a host computer.

link A "hot spot" in a hypertext document or file that has been coded to connect the reader to another location within the document or file or to another document or file.

Listproc A program that allows electronic mail messages directed to a designated address to be sent automatically to all subscribers. *See also* Listserv, MajorDomo.

Listserv Similar to Listproc, this is a type of software that allows electronic mail messages directed to a designated address to be sent automatically to all subscribers to the list. While not entirely accurate, many users use the term "listserv" generically to refer to all types of Internet mailing lists. *See also* Listproc, MajorDomo.

Local Area Network *See* LAN.

Lynx A text-only browser that allows users to view files on the World Wide Web using standard text features. Typographical elements such as fonts, emphasis, and colors and features such as tables and graphics are stripped from the files; however, users may download graphics and other multimedia elements for viewing in other applications.

MajorDomo One of several types of programs that allow mailing lists to be set up and maintained to support the dissemination of electronic mail messages to subscribers. *See also* Listproc, Listserv.

microcomputer See PC.

mirror A site that copies, or "mirrors," information originally posted or published on another site. Mirrors are usually created in order to limit traffic on the original site or to foster quicker access to information from a remote site.

modem Modulate/Demodulate. A hardware device that converts data from analog to digital or from digital to analog, thus allowing communication of electronic files between computers using standard telephone lines designed for voice communication.

Modulate/Demodulate *See* modem.

MOO MUD, Object-Oriented. A form of MUD (*which see*), used for role-playing games, synchronous conferencing, and distance education applications.

Motion Picture Experts Group *See* MPEG.

mouse A computer input device that allows the user to control the movements of a pointer on the computer screen in order to activate information or perform other actions.

MPEG Motion Picture Experts Group. A standard for the compression of video files. *See also* GIF, JPEG.

MUD Multi-User Dungeon, Domain, or Dimension. A form of the *Dungeons and Dragons* game originally developed for multiple users on the Internet. Forms of MUDs include MOOs (*which see*), MUSEs, MUCKs, etc.

MUD, Object-Oriented *See* MOO.

multimedia A mixture of various types of media, including audio, video, graphics, and text.

Multi-User Dungeon, Domain, or Dimension *See* MUD.

name anchor In Hypertext Markup Language, a reference to a specific location within a document or WWW page, usually referred to in the address by a pound sign (#) and reference name or keyword directly following the address of the document. For example, http://www.cas.usf.edu/english/walker/papers/rhetoric.html#massy refers to a specific reference ("#massy") designated in HTML by the tag pair <A NAME=" ">. . . </A>.

Net Short for the Internet, hence the initial capital letter.

online The state during which a computer is connected to and sharing information or programs with another computer or a server. Also sometimes used to designate any work or information on a computer. Online should not be hyphenated.

page On the WWW, a page is a document or file with a single URL, regardless of its length.

path The route taken through the directory structure of a host computer to access a specific file or program.

PC Personal computer. Used to designate a desktop computer that serves a single user, usually with an IBM-compatible platform. *Microcomputer* is a synonym.

Persistent Uniform Resource Locator *See* PURL.

personal computer *See* PC.

platform Usually the designation of the specific operating system used by a computer, such as DOS, Windows95, Macintosh, Unix, and the like.

plug-ins Software applications designed to work with other programs, such as Internet browsers, to extend their capabilities. For example, plug-ins may enable a user to play audio or video files included within hypermedia documents on the World Wide Web.

point-and-click A means of inputting information into a computer by using a mouse or other pointing device to move a cursor, or arrow, on the screen and then depressing a button to designate the desired location or action on the screen.

Point-to-Point Protocol *See* PPP.

port A number that identifies a specific channel or access location at a given IP address.

PPP Point-to-Point Protocol. The standard for transmission of information on the Internet, allowing for multiple processes to occur on a single line or connection. Users connected via PPP may use various client programs residing on the user's local host, or PC, such as browser software. *See also* SLIP.

protocol A set of rules agreed upon for performing various tasks on the Internet. Common protocols include File Transfer Protocol (FTP), Hypertext Transfer Protocol (HTTP), gopher protocols, and telnet protocols.

PURL Persistent Uniform Resource Locator. A form of fictitious Internet address developed by the Online Computer Library Center (OCLC) to allow for stable Internet addresses.

running head An abbreviated and informative version of the title of a document. Running heads are located in the header of every page of a printed document.

search engine A program that allows users to search for information or files at various locations using keyword searches and, usually, Boolean operators. Some search engines search specific sites or types of files; other search engines will search all information on the Internet.

Serial Line Internet Protocol *See* SLIP.

server A computer, or host, that allocates resources and supports the sharing of information among various computers on a network.

SGML Standard Generalized Markup Language. An international standard for formatting a text. SGML is particularly useful for the electronic storage and transmission of files across platforms because it is system- and device-independent.

shell The user interface that executes operating system commands. On the Internet, it often refers to a type of account that allows users to access files and execute commands on the host computer through a command-line interface (*which see*).

site On the Internet, a specific domain or Internet address.

SLIP Serial Line Internet Protocol. Not as stable as a PPP connection, a SLIP connection allows a dial-in user to run client programs, such as a Web browser, on the Internet. *See also* PPP.

soft return A return that a word processor inserts automatically at the end of the line when the text on that line reaches the right margin. Users should not rely on soft returns to end paragraphs and begin new ones. *See also* hard return.

software Usually, a computer program that instructs the system to perform certain actions to input, retrieve, manipulate, process, output, or store data items. Software controls the operating environment and provides an interface for the user to communicate with the computer in various ways.

Standard Generalized Markup Language *See* SGML.

synchronous Used to designate communication or commands that take place simultaneously and appear on the user's screen in succession. Internet chat rooms and MUDs are forms of synchronous communication sites.

tags Commands enclosed within angle brackets that designate various hypertextual features in Hypertext Markup Language.

TCP/IP Transmission Control Protocol/Internet Protocol. A protocol developed by the U.S. Department of Defense that establishes rules, or protocols, for the transmission of data packets (usually bytes of information) among remote computers of various types.

telnet An Internet protocol that permits remote access to programs that reside on another computer. Telnet sites may require the user to have an account on the host machine; many telnet sites also allow for guest accounts.

Transmission Control Protocol/Internet Protocol *See* TCP/IP.

Uniform Resource Name *See* URN.

UNIX An operating system used by many Internet host machines that accommodates multiple users and multitasking

URL Uniform Resource Locator. The Internet address used by browser software to connect to sites on the World Wide Web. A URL usually includes a designation of the protocol, a domain name, directories, and a file name.

URN Uniform Resource Name. A unique name assigned to an electronic file that remains the same regardless of the address or location of the file, thus allowing for more accurate search capabilities.

Virtual Reality Modeling Language *See* VRML.

VRML Virtual Reality Modeling Language. A language used to encode and communicate 3-D graphics files among various platforms. It requires a VRML-enabled browser, that is, a browser capable of recognizing and responding to VRML commands.

WAIS Wide Area Information Server. A server offering a method of searching the full text of documents and files on the Internet for keywords.

WAN Wide Area Network. Similar to a LAN, a network of computers linked together to share information, files, programs, or hardware and served by a host machine, usually a minicomputer or mainframe, that allocates resources. Unlike LANs, however, WANs often link computers over a large geographic area, including worldwide links. Unlike the Internet, however, WANs are limited to use only by employees or other persons authorized to access the server. *See also* Intranet.

Web Short for the World Wide Web, hence the initial capital letter.

Web site A Web site is a specific location or a specific group of related files, usually within a single directory or subdirectory, on the World Wide Web.

Wide Area Information Server *See* WAIS.

Wide-Area Network *See* WAN.

World Wide Web *See* WWW.

WWW World Wide Web. Also known as the Web, the various forms of documents and files transmitted on the Internet and capable of being accessed using a browser. The WWW is not the same thing as the Internet but rather a user-friendly system of organizing information on the Internet for remote access.

XML eXtensible Markup Language. A version of SGML that allows Web page designers to create customized tags to define functionality. *See also* SGML.

INDEX

Italic page references indicate illustrations.